Kalamazoo Daily Gazette

Concise history of the fire and water department of the village of Kalamazoo

From its incorporation in 1843 to 1881

Kalamazoo Daily Gazette

Concise history of the fire and water department of the village of Kalamazoo
From its incorporation in 1843 to 1881

ISBN/EAN: 9783741181733

Manufactured in Europe, USA, Canada, Australia, Japa

Cover: Foto ©ninafisch / pixelio.de

Manufactured and distributed by brebook publishing software
(www.brebook.com)

Kalamazoo Daily Gazette

Concise history of the fire and water department of the village of Kalamazoo

CONCISE HISTORY

OF THE

FIRE AND WATER DEPARTMENT,

OF THE

VILLAGE OF KALAMAZOO, MICH.,

FROM ITS INCORPORATION IN 1843 TO 1881,

COMPILED FROM THE

VILLAGE RECORDS,

BY A

SPECIAL COMMITTEE

————Appointed by the Village Board, February 17th, 1881.-————

KALAMAZOO:

DAILY GAZETTE BOOK AND JOB DEPARTMENT,

1881.

*To the Honorable, the President and Trustees of the Village
of Kalamazoo:*

Your committee, appointed February 17, 1881, "to collect and compile a
history" of our Fire and Water interests and enterprises since the incorporation
of our Village, in April, 1843, till April, 1881, have now performed their allotted
task, and the result is herewith submitted.

It is proper to say, that, though great care has been taken to be absolutely
accurate in dates, and in the statement of expenditures, it is possible a few un-
important errors may be found.

That just credit may be given to each member of the committee, for his individual share of the work, (for all have worked) the undersigned takes occasion
to say, that Frank Little, Esq., is the author of the introductory chapter and the
compiler of the "Chronicle of Events" from the beginning, in 1843, to May 12,
1869—a labor that required great good judgment and painstaking patience.

That the undersigned, continued the "Chronicle of Events" from the last
mentioned date to April 15, 1872; writing, also, the "Intermediate Chapter," introductory to the "Water Works Period," the chapter on the "Geological Relations of the Well," and the "Closing Chapter."

That Mr. W. R. Coats furnished the chapter on the "Construction of the
Well" now in use at the Water Works.

That Mr. Fred. Cellem, aided by Mr. Jas. W. Hopkins, Village Clerk, continued the "Chronicle of Events" from April 17, till their close April 18, 1881.
Mr. Cellem is also the compiler, of the "Financial Exhibit of the Fire and
Water Department," for the last twelve years—covering the financial history
of the Water Works, year by year, since their beginning. This has been a work
requiring great care and labor; and its results are believed to be as nearly accurate as it is possible, now, to make them.

To Mr. Chandler, Engineer at the Water Works, we are indebted for the
"History of Machinery,," and for the exceedingly valuable tables, showing "Lo-
cation of all Water Mains," "Fire Hydrants," and "Water Gates," and the
"Pumping Record" of the Water Works for the last year.

It is proper to add, also, that Mr. Geo. Nitschke furnished, at the request of
the undersigned, the skeleton "map" showing all our sources of natural water
supply, and the "Geological Diagram" illustrative of the source and volume of
the water we now use.

Hoping that the results of our joint labors will meet your approval and be of
service to our people in the future, I am, very respectfully,

FOSTER PRATT,
Chairman Committee.

Kalamazoo, June 15, 1881.

ERRATA.

Page 9—4th Paragraph: For "'53—Oct. 1," read '*55—Sept. 29;* and transfer the entire paragraph to page 11, to follow that dated, "'55—Sept. 8."

Page 17—1st Paragraph: Strike out all after "should," in the middle of third line, and add so as to read: *"should raise twenty-five pounds of steam, per square inch, from cold water, in ten minutes."*

Page 61—8th Line: Strike out the words "average annual," so that it will read: *"Net cost of Fire Department for 12 years, $42,013.70.*

A CONCISE HISTORY

OF THE

FIRE DEP'T AND WATER WORKS

OF KALAMAZOO VILLAGE,

FROM APRIL 10, 1843, TO APRIL 18, 1881,

At a special meeting of the President and Trustees of the village of Kalamazoo, held at Corporation Hall, Thursday evening, February 17th, 1881, Trustee Clarage, chairman of the standing Committee on Fire and Water, moved the following resolution, which was unanimously adopted:

"RESOLVED, That a committee of six, to be appointed by the chair,
"be requested to collect and compile a history of our water works,
"from their inception to the present time, with such tabulated statistics
"as they may deem proper or valuable, and present the same to the board
"at their earliest convenience, for such further action as may be deemed
"proper."

In pursuance of the foregoing resolution, the President, Hon. Peyton Ranney, appointed as such committee:

Dr. Foster Pratt, Ex-President, Chairman.

Frank Little, Ex-Clerk.

Frederick Cellem, Ex-Clerk.

William R. Coats, Ex-Water Commissioner.

George H. Chandler, Chief Engineer Water Works.

James W. Hopkins, present Village Clerk.

The committee as above named, met at the council room, Corporation Hall, Monday, February 21st, 1881, and arranged a subdivision of the work assigned them, so as to secure as far as possible a full and careful investigation of all the prominent facts and incidents bearing upon the subject of fire protection, and of water supply for the village of Kalamazoo, from the date of incorporation, in April, 1843, down to the present time.

The committee were at the outset fully impressed with the importance and magnitude of the work assigned them. They realized that a faithful collation and recital of facts such they hoped to be able to present, and in the form and manner as agreed upon, would be of value and interest, not only to those who still remain, of the noble band of Michigan's early pioneers, who laid the foundations of our beautiful village of Kalamazoo, but also to those who should first learn of the incidents narrated by a perusal of these pages, and to the generations that shall come after.

It was determined by the committee that, so far as possible, everything pertaining to the subjects in hand should be arranged in chronological order, so that the inception, and subsequent development in the various directions indicated, might be clearly and intelligently traced.

The committee also found that the two questions of fire protection and water supply were so inseparably related, and the one so entirely dependent upon the other, that they should be treated as a unit in this investigation. Furthermore, while this sketch is continuous in the recital of events, yet in view of what has transpired, the whole subject has been naturally divided into two distinct periods of time. At the first, in the early settlement of the village, any citizen could secure excellent water upon his premises by simply digging a well, varying from ten to twenty-four feet in depth. This water was usually found at a uniform level, in strata of sand and gravel, and in ample supply for all ordinary domestic purposes.

As population increased, and fires became somewhat frequent, the necessity of making some provision for a larger supply of water than could be drawn from a common well or cistern, for extinguishing fires, became apparent to every householder.

The Arcadia Creek, a small and beautiful stream, entered the village from the southwest, nearly upon the then central dividing line of the corporation, and flowed easterly about one block north of and parallel with Main street, to the Kalamazoo River. [For a better understanding of the natural resources for water supply, reference is had to the diagram accompanying this report.]

The Arcadia, having its source at an elevation of some 100 feet above the outlet, had at an early day attracted the attention of persons interested in securing water power for various uses; and, while the supply was not adequate for propelling heavy machinery, still title had been secured by individuals to the so-called "privileges" along its banks, and it was being utilized for many enterprises, such as turning lathes, chair and cabinet works, planing mills, and wool-carding machines.

Thus it will be seen that the village authorities could not legally divert the stream of the Arcadia, or appropriate its waters to the detriment of any of the several mill owners along its banks; and had to be content with the waste, or surplus water, after it had passed the several mills.

The Swazey wool-carding mill, located on the south side of Main street, one block east of J. L. Sebring & Co.'s elevator, was propelled by water brought from the Arcadia in a race which crossed Main street upon the west line of Porter street. A flume was constructed in the race close to the sidewalk on the north side of Main street, with a gate, which, upon being shut down, furnished a sufficient depth of water to supply the "bucket brigade," who dipped their pails in the flume.

Arrangements of like character were made at intervals up the Arcadia for the same purpose, which were used for supplying water in pails, and afterwards enlarged for taking suction with fire engines.

The Michigan Central Railroad Company, upon the establishment of their depot, laid a line of wooden pipe, on railroad land, up the Arcadia to a point of sufficient elevation to supply water to the one tank then at the depot.

Superintendent Brooks, of the railroad company, offered the overflow from this tank to the village, whereupon the *first reservoir* or cistern was built in the Court House yard, and this surplus water was discharged into the reservoir through wooden pipes laid from the depot.

The precise length of time this overflow from the depot was distributed in the manner above indicated, the committee have been unable to ascertain, but we find this fact recorded, that in the fall of 1854, Mr. Geo. N. Bolles erected a dam upon the Arcadia between Rose and Burdick streets, built a shop fronting on Eleanor street, and put in machinery for running a lathe, sawing and woodworking; and in 1860, we find upon the journal of the village a memorandum of an agreement on the part of Bolles to pump water into the reservoir from his shop on the Arcadia.

Iron pipes were laid from Bolles shop, soon after, to the reservoir and a force pump was provided by the village to be used in filling the reservoir.

Subsequently, the Bolles dam was removed, and pumping was done at the Lawrence and Gale foundry until the introduction of the Holly system, in 1869. (This foundry stood upon the ground now occupied by the Kalamazoo Iron Works of Lawrence & Chapin.

As will be seen by an examination of the following sketch, after the construction of the Main street reservoirs, and the organization of an efficient fire department, with three engines, hooks and ladders, and other apparatus, the situation remained practically undisturbed, with the exception of extensive explorations in various directions in 1866 and 1868, for a general water supply, until the construction of the Holly water works in 1869, which forms a new and distinct era in the history of this great and important enterprise of water supply and fire protection in Kalamazoo.

CHRONICLE OF EVENTS.

1843—APRIL 10.   First charter election under the act of incorporation of the village of Kalamazoo.

Inspectors of the election, Henry Gilbert and Richard S. Gage, Justices of the Peace, and Volney Hascall, Township Clerk.

Trustees elected: Hosea B. Huston, Hiram Arnold, Abraham Cahill, Wm. H. Welch, Lewis R. Davis, Warren Burrill, Caleb Sherman.   Hosea B. Huston became president of the village by election of the board of trustees.

1843—JUNE 5.   Village ordinance passed, requiring all household-holders, storekeepers and occupants of all buildings in the village, to provide themselves with two ladders, one for use on the ground, and the other on the roof; also two pails or buckets, all to be marked with the owners' name, and to be kept and used exclusively for the purpose of extinguishing fires.

1844—OCT. 7.—Ordinance passed prohibiting the kindling of bonfires, leaves, or the burning of any substance in the streets from sundown until sunrise; or the firing of any anvil, cannon, or other ordinance within the village limits.

1844—DEC. 14.   N. A. Balch, L. W. Whitcomb, Chas. E. Stuart, L. H. Trask and Israel Kellogg appointed fire wardens, to attend, take charge of, and control the persons present at all fires in the village.

1844—DEC. 14. Fire wardens authorized to expend five dollars out any public funds on hand, and solicit from citizens the additional amount needed, " for the purchase of a good and sufficient FIRE HOOK for the use of the village." (This fire hook is believed to be the first implement purchased by the village for use in extinguishing fires.)

1846—MAR. 11. " Kalamazoo Hook and Ladder Company " organized. Alex. J. Sheldon foreman. [From the village records, this appears to be the first organization of a fire company in the village.]

'46—APRIL 10. An appropriation of $59.03 out of the village treasury for the purchase of " hooks, ladders, ropes and other articles for the use of the Hook and Ladder Company."

'46—APRIL 30. Alex. J. Sheldon chosen chief engineer of the new fire department.

Meeting of citizens and resolutions passed, requesting the President and Trustees to purchase 100 fire buckets.

'46—MAY 4. Chief engineer authorized to call a mass meeting of citizens of the village to consider the propriety of levying a tax for the purchase of 100 fire buckets and other apparatus for the fire department.

'46—JULY 6. Wagon, or truck, and apparatus for the Hook and Ladder Company purchased.

1847—APRIL 6. Penalty imposed for taking away or using any articles belonging to the fire department without consent of the chief engineer.

'47—MAY 3. Petition of citizens "requesting the Board of Trustees to levy a tax for the purchase of a Fire Engine and apparatus. Petition referred to a committee, who recommended a tax of $1,000 to procure a suitable engine, which report was accepted.

1848—MAY 1. Messrs. D. S. Walbridge, Horace Mower and T. P. Sheldon appointed a committee to consider the necessity of levying a tax for the purchase of a fire engine. They advised that $700 be raised. The report was laid upon the table.

'48—Oct. 2. A tax of three mills on the dollar ordered, to assist in the purchase of a fire engine.

A committee of two was chosen at the same meeting of the board, "to confer with all persons interested as owners in the "waters of the Arcadia Creek, and to ascertain whether the "water can be obtained for the use of the village in case "of fire."

'48—Nov. 6. The order to levy a tax of three mills on the dollar, for the purchase of a fire engine (passed Oct. 2, '48), rescinded.

1850—Feb. 5. Ordinance of June 5, '43, requiring citizens to keep ladders and pails for fire purposes, repealed.

[Insurance policies at this time contained a clause, requiring policy holders to conform strictly to all ordinances of the village for extinguishing fires, or policies should be void. As but few, comparatively, were complying with the strict letter of law, to save the policies, the ordinance was repealed.]

The Marshal was instructed to procure six ladders, at the public expense, for use in extinguishing fires.

'50—Feb. 9. A fire occurred, destroying all buildings on the north side of Main street, where now stands the Burdick House and the buildings next west of it—the northeast corner building on Rose street alone escaping. These buildings were occupied by five stores, three carpenter shops, and the Telegraph newspaper office.

'50—Mar. 9. "Rescue Hook and Ladder Company" organized, 41 members. Benj. F. Orcutt, afterwards sheriff of the county, was chosen foreman.

'50—Aug. 7. Messrs. Alex. Buell, L. H. Trask and William E. White were appointed a committee "to examine and report upon the probable expense of bringing WATER into the village to supply the wants of the citizens' thereof."

1851—April 26. The Michigan Central Railroad Co., having established a tank at their depot, which was supplied with a continuous stream of water through wooden pipes, had an overflow of waste water, which the company offered to the village authorities free of cost for the purpose of extinguishing fires. Whereupon, Messrs. Wm. R. Watson and Alex. Buell were appointed a committee to confer with the railroad company in reference to the privilege tendered, of using such surplus water.

'51—APRIL 28. Messrs. Watson and Buell, committee as above, reported "that Supt. Brooks, of the Michigan Central Railroad, would donate said surplus water to the village for the uses as stated;" which offer was accepted with thanks by the board; and the marshal was instructed "to provide for taking said water to a point in Kalamazoo avenue, and to connect with the Arcadia." [This plan, or direction, to the marshal was never carried out, but in a short time a reservoir was constructed in the Court House yard; wooden pipes were laid from the rail-road tanks, and the waste water water was discharged into said reservoir. A Mr. Bugbee rented power of Trowbridge & Near-pass, tenants of Turner, White & Co., foundrymen, and bored the logs which were used as above described.]

'51—MAY 1st. Allen's mill—widely known as the "Black Mill"—near the M. C. R. R. depot was burned, causing a loss of about $10,000.

'51—MAY 2. Citizens' meeting held and petition signed, request-ing village board to purchase a fire engine, and provide a build-ing for storing same.

'51—MAY 5. Petition from citizens' meeting in reference to fire engine referred to special committee, Messrs. Kellogg, Watson Clark.

'51—MAY 5. White & Turner's foundry and machine shop, (where Lawrence & Chapin's building now stands) was burned, loss about $8,000.

'51—MAY 19. The special committee of the Board made a report recommending that a RESERVOIR be constructed in the court house'yard, with hydrants at the corner of Main and Burdick and Main and Portage streets; that a FIRE ENGINE, not exceeding in cost $800, be purchased and a house be provided for the same; which report was adopted. (Only the court yard reser-voir was constructed in the summer of 1851. It was first sup-plied with water through wooden pipes laid from the tank of the M. C. R. R. Afterwards, water was pumped from the Ar-cadia creek, by Geo. M. Bolles at his shop, and by Arms & Co. and Gale & Lawrence at the foundry and machine shop.)

'51—JUNE 2. Messrs. W. R. Watson, Israel Kellogg, and L. H. Trask were made a permanent committee on "WATER WORKS,

"and all matters relating to the Arcadia Creek, and all waters
"in the corporation."

'51—July 7. Village ordinance No. 28 passed, organizing and
regulating a fire department.

'51—Sept. 17. "Old blast furnace," on the east side of the river
and below the site of Riverside cemetery, was burned.

1852—Jan'y 5. A vote of thanks passed by the village board to J.
J. Perrin, Henry Colt and Moses Ward for personal skill and
bravery in extinguishing a fire in the loft of Parsons & Woods'
dry goods store, north side of Main street.

'52—"Fireman's Hall Association" organized and building erected. (The U. S. Post-Office is now kept in the same building,
April, 1881.)

1853—Feb'y 10. B. S. Gleason, of the Kalamazoo House, granted
permission to "tap the water works (Main street hydrant) and
"use so much of the waste water as he shall see fit" (below the
tanks).

'53—May —. M. C. R. R. depot, Henry Cock & Co.'s warehouse,
and several neighboring saloons were burned. One life lost.

'53—June 6. R. S. Gage and J. C. Hays appointed a committee
to procure a suitable piece of ground upon which to build an
engine house and shed for hooks and ladders.

'53—July 8. Eleven hundred dollars appropriated by the President and Trustees for the purchase of a fire engine and apparatus. Allen Potter authorized to buy the machine.

Marshal ordered to erect a shed for the storage of hook
and ladders.

Messrs. Whitcomb, Potter and Winslow appointed a committee to consider "expediency of building cisterns in suitable
"localities of sufficient capacity to hold a supply of water for
"fire emergencies."

The committee made report recommending that five cisterns be constructed, to be placed as follows: One fronting the
residences each of Gov. Ransom, Dr. Abbott, N. A. Balch, E.
Hoskins and Ira Burdick.

These cisterns were to be supplied with water (through
small lead pipes) from the court yard reservoir, and to be of the

capacity of 150 to 20C barrels each, and to cost $25 each. (They were never constructed.)

'53—JULY 25. A small fire engine, "Cataract," purchased of Messrs. Ransom and Arnold, with a small amount of hose belonging to it; all for the sum of $129.00. Also use of another small engine, "Star," secured from same parties whenever necessity should arise. (These are the first fire engines used for extinguishing fires. They were bought by Messrs. Ransom and Arnold for use in their distillery. Same building now used by George Judge as a malt house.)

'53—AUG. 19. Allen Potter authorized to purchase a Rochester fire engine, at a cost of $900; and 266 feet of leather hose at seventy five cents per foot.

'53—SEPT. 5. Rescue Fire Company, No. 1, organized with fifty-one members. A. G. Hopkins, foreman. (The title of this company was afterwards changed to "Bur Oak Engine Company, No. 1.")

'53—OCT. 1. North side of Main street, west of Burdick House up to Rose street—the corner store on Rose street again escaping—all burned.

'53—OCT. 25. Additional apparatus procured for the hook and ladder company.

53—DEC. 22. Fire engine purchased of Wright Bros., Rochester, N. Y., at a cost of $1,050, with 200 feet of hose. Same was formally presented to and accepted by Bur Oak Engine Company, No. 1.

1854—JAN'Y 5. Hose cart, axes, &c., purchased for the fire department.

'54—FEB'Y 20 Organization of "Excelsior Fire Company, Engine No. 2." Geo. H. Gale, foreman; 27 men. Engine "Cataract" put in custody of said company.

Messrs. Whitcomb and Winslow appointed a committee by the Board to determine the expediency of tapping conduit to reservoir in court yard for other uses than fire supply.

'54—MARCH 25. Engine house and cistern constructed in rear of new Firemen's Hall, for use of Bur Oak Co., No. 1.

'54—MAR. 27. Permission given to Mr. Hays to use water from the reservoir for mixing mortar, provided that he shall construct a cistern at the junction of Main and Portage street, free of cost, except materials, and of the capacity of 200 barrels.

1854—APRIL 11.   A juvenile fire company organized with twenty members.   Andrew J. Clark foreman.   [The engine "Star," formed the nucleus of this company.]

'54—MAY 15.   Excelsior Fire Company, No. 2, petitioned the village board, asking for a new engine for their company.   Petition referred to committee on fire and water.

Gov. Ransom, chairman of the committee, made following report: " Excelsior Fire Company, No. 2, is composed of young " active, energetic and efficient residents of this village.   They " are respectable, responsible men of correct habits, and proper " persons to have charge of an engine.   The prayer of petition- " ers should be granted, and one thousand dollars appropriated " for the purchase of an engine for said company."

Report as above accepted and subsequently adopted.

'54—JUNE 15.   Village bond issued for the sum of one thousand dollars, for the purchase of Excelsior Engine, No. 2, Button machine.

'54—AUG. 15.   A plat of ground on the west side of Burdick street, next south of and adjoining Firemen's Hall, bought of Miss Susan Rice for $1,500.   [This is the present site of Corporation Hall.]

'54—SEPT. 1.   A small wooden building was moved on the northeast corner of Corporation Hall lot, and fitted up as an engine house for Excelsior Fire Company, No. 2.

1855—FEB'Y 12.   A petition of S. S. Cobb and others was received by the board in reference to water supply.

A committee consisting of Messrs. Ransom, Kendall and Clapham was appointed " to make a survey and ascertain the " probable cost of procuring WATER for the use of the village."

1855—APRIL 3.   The Committee on Fire and Water were requested " to ascertain the expense of constructing five reservoirs, and for taking and carrying water to and from the same."

The committee reported, recommending " the construction " of a series of cisterns of the capacity of 200 barrels each, on " the line of South street, at each crossing of streets running "north and south."

Six hundred feet of leading leather hose purchased, and a hose company organized.

'55—JUNE 4. Committee on Fire and Water authorized to invite proposals for the construction of six cisterns on South St. and two on Main St., one at the crossing of Burdick street and the other at the junction of Portage with Main. The committee were instructed to enter immediately upon the work of building such of the above cisterns as they shall deem of immediate importance. [The South street cisterns were never constructed, but the Main street reservoirs were built in the summer of 1855, and the old Court House reservoir was rebuilt.]

'55—JULY 2. Messrs. Gleason & Simth, of the Kalamazoo House, asked permission of the Board to *tap* the Main street reservoir, and use the surplus water.

'55—JULY 25. A contract entered into with Messrs. VanRiper and Buell for a town clock, with a fire alarm attachment. [The clock when received, was placed in the tower of the Baptist church.]

'55—SEPT. 8. The Main street reservoirs at Burdick and Portage streets completed; also court yard reservoir reconstructed. Cost of reservoirs $830.

'55—OCT. 1. Penalty imposed upon all persons who should " re- " move any plug, open or close any gate; or in any way injure " the water works, logs or cisterns belonging to said water " works."

'55—DEC. 10. Village Board voted to refund the amount paid by Excelsior Company, interest upon a loan negotiated by said company for the purchase of hose cart, &c., and assumed the balance of indebtedness due by the company.

1856—SEPT. 22. The sum of $65 allowed Excelsior Engine Company, No. 2, for a balance on hose cart, &c., previously purchased by them Said cart and apparatus to become the property of the village.

'56—OCT. 15. A store and lot on the South side of Main street, known as the " Tannehill store," and nearly opposite the residence of W. G. Pattison, bought of S. H. Wattles, for an engine house. Cost $1,700. (The upper story of this building was subsequently used as a place of meeting and office of the President and Trustees.)

1857—MARCH —. Dr. Chas. V. Mottram's large unfinished house on Burdick street, just south of site of Corporation Hall. Total loss by fire.

'57—JULY 6. It would appear from certain incidents that water was being pumped at Geo. N. Bolles shop, on the Arcadia, into the court yard reservoir, and from thence by the connections into the two reservoirs on Main street at this time; but the proof of this is not clear until 1860.

'57—JULY 16. A hose cart purchased for Burr Oak engine company No. 1, cost $150. [No entry appears upon the journal in 1858 bearing in the remotest degree upon the subjects under consideration. This is somewhat remarkable.]

1858—FEB'Y 10. Center (unfinished) of the north Asylum building burnt.

'58—DEC. 15. W. W. Allcott's steam flouring mill, north of M. C. R. R. on Burdick street, burned.

1859—JULY 11. New fire engine purchased for Burr Oak Co., No. 1, at a cost of $1,500.

'59—AUG. 19. The Committee on Fire and Water were authorized to take such measures as they should deem advisable or necessary, with reference to sinking an artesian well to supply the village with water.

'59—OCT. 8. "Old River House," near Main street river bridge, on the north side of the street, burnt.

1860—MAR. 12. Germania Fire Engine Co., No. 3 organized; Nicholas Baumann foreman. Organization accepted by the Board.

A reorganization was had of Empire Hook and Ladder Co., No. 1.

'60—APRIL 2. Jas. A. Walter authorized by the Board to purchase, upon six months' credit of the village, 1,000 feet of three inch iron water pipe. [This pipe was laid from Bolles' shop on the Arcadia to the court yard reservoir.]—See Annual Report, April 15, 1861.

'60—MAY 12. Contract entered into (or renewal) with Geo. N.

Bolles for pumping water into the court yard and Main street reservoirs. The force pump used was furnished by and belonged to the village.

'60—Aug. 15. A brick hose tower ordered to be erected on the rear portion of the corporation lot, on Burdick street.

1862—Mar. 10. The Chief Engineer of the Fire Department made report to the Board in reference to apparatus belonging to the village for extinguishing fires: Three fire engines, three hose carts, one hook and ladder truck, 1,800 feet of available hose; also, an aggregate of 148 men belonging to the several fire companies.

Ordinance No. 32 passed for the prevention of fires, and for the regulation of the fire department.

1863—May 6. Committee on Fire and Water authorized to sell Germania engine No. 3.

'63—June 15. First purchase of rubber hose.

'63—July 6. The Committee on Fire and Water were authorized to purchase a "Button" fire engine, in all respects equal to and similar to engine No. 2, at a cost of $845. [This new engine was for Germania Co. No. 3.]

'63—Sept. 16. The Village Board were petitioned to demolish the Bolles dam, to abate overflow of water upon private property. Laid upon the table.

1864—July 6. W. W. Alcott made a proposition to the Board, that he would enter into an engagement to supply the village with an ample supply of pure water from a spring located about two and one-fourth miles south of Main street, near the present site of the paper mill. [No contract was ever made.]

'64—Oct. 3. The Committee on Fire and Water were authorized to procure an immediate supply of water for the use of the fire department.

1865—Oct. 23. E. W. Morgan, of Ann Arbor, made a proposal to the Village Board to sell the property at the head of Lovel street, known as the Eames' water power, to the village for the sum of $10,000. This was referred to the Fire and Water Committee, who made report recommending the purchase.

'65—Nov. 2. President H. G. Wells was appointed a committee to engage a competent civil engineer to survey the Eames' water power, Alcott spring, or other source of water supply for the village.

1866—JAN'Y 15.   E. S. Chesbrough, civil engineer of Chicago, made careful surveys and estimates of a pure water supply from Eames' power, Alcott springs, and Loring lake.   The engineer's report is entered at large upon the village journal under date of January 15, 1866.   Of the three sources examined, the engineer recommended "Alcott spring" as the more feasible, and less expensive than either of the others.

Messrs. Jonathan Parsons and Henry Bishop were appointed a committee to confer with Mr. W. W. Alcott in reference to procuring a water supply from his spring.

'66—FEB'Y 9.   The Committee on Fire and Water were instructed to put down six inch iron water pipes in Main and Burdick streets, to the extent that it was proposed to pave said streets with " Nicholson pavement."   [This pipe was laid on Main street, from Rose to the east side of the Kalamazoo House, and on Burdick street from the M. C. R. R. depot to the south side of Corporation Hall.]

'66—MAY 8.   New ladders, truck and apparatus provided for Empire Hook and Ladder Company; cost, $1,000.

1867—JAN'Y 26.   Plans and specifications adopted for the erection of "Corporation Hall" for fire engines, fire department, and public offices of the village.

'67—MAR. 4.   The following bids for construction of "Corporation Hall," as per plans adopted, were received: Alex Cameron's bid, $14,500; L. H. Trask's bid, $16,750; Hays & Hopkins' bid, $17,087.50.

'67—APRIL 22.   Contract entered into with Bush & Paterson for the building of Corporation Hall, for the sum of $15,500.

Hon. Allen Potter appointed as superintendent to overlook the work in its progress.

'67—Nov. 9.   Village ordinance passed authorizing the President and Trustees to contract for the establishment of hydraulic works, either by a private company or at the public expense, for supplying Kalamazoo village with water, and to purchase water pipes, engines, and all the necessary outfit; also, to regulate charges and distribution of water to citizens of the village.

1868—SEPT. 26. Resolutions passed at a citizens' meeting at the Court House, urging the President and Trustees to provide *at once* for the introduction of water into the village.

'68—OCT. 5. Messrs. H. F. Cock, Allen Potter, L. H. Trask, S. S. Cobb and C. L. Cobb were appointed a committee to examine into, make surveys, and determine the best plan for supplying pure water to the village.

'68—NOV. 2. Lawrence & Gale gave notice, declining to pump water hereafter into corporation reservoirs.

'68—NOV. 7. Contract entered into with Lawrence & Gale to pump water into reservoirs until the spring of 1869, at $25 per month.

'68—DEC. 14. H. F. Cock, chairman of the committee of five, chosen October 5, 1868, in reference to supply of water for the village made report, with recommendations substantially as follows:

A purchase of the Cold Stream mill water power at a cost of $35,000.

The "Holly system" of water supply and fire protection, superceding fire engines and reservoirs.

Estimated cost of water wheel, pumps and machinery of the capacity of 2,000,000 gallons per day, $15,000.

Twelve and one-half miles of pipe of the various sizes needed, with hydrants, gates, etc., $112,129.

Making a grand total as then estimated of $162,129.00.

The committee also reported the necessity of sewerage, and its probable cost from $100,000 to $500,000.

1869—JAN'Y 4. Messrs. Bixby, Cobb and House chosen a committee to select grounds, obtain proposals and estimates of the cost of sinking an artesian well in the village.

'69—FEB'Y 17. Messrs. Phelps and House appointed a committee to purchase a lot of N. Benedict for location of water works on Eleanor street, at a cost not exceeding $2,500.

'69—MAR. 1. The committee as above reported that they had purchased said lot on Eleanor street at the sum of $2,300.

'69—APRIL 17. A disastrous fire, having its origin in the Stevens boarding house on Academy street, consumed a number of buildings, spending its full force unchecked so far as the efforts

acceptance of the machinery above described the village authorities were to pay ten thousand dollars on the 10th of September, 1869, at which time the works were to be in readiness for public test.

The company were to furnish sixteen double hydrants at $50 each, and sixteen single hydrants at $40 each. They also stipulated that the boiler should stand a pressure of twenty-five pounds to the square inch, and that steam from cold water should be raised in ten minutes.

'69—MAY 10.   A special election was held to provide, by the issuing of bonds of the village, to secure a supply of water for fire protection, for raising the sum of twenty-five thousand dollars in equal payments annually of five thousand dollars.

'69—MAY 12.   The Committee on Fire and Water authorized to contract with Wm. Smith, of Pittsburg, for water pipe for street mains.

'69—MAY 18.   Committee on Fire and Water instructed to ascertain the amount and character of water obtainable on the Eleanor street lot, by digging a well near the Arcadia.

Eight inch iron pipe ordered to connect the proposed Water Works on Eleanor street, with the pipes now laid under the paved streets.

'69—MAY 24.   One hundred dollars ordered to be paid to Carl Rudow, fireman, for injuries received while bravely doing duty at the recent fire on Academy and Main streets, and for consequent loss of time

Engine and Pumps ordered to be located on the Eleanor street lot.

Trustee Phelps employed to superintend said work.

'69—MAY 26.   Remonstrance drawn and circulated by Dr. Pratt, and signed by one hundred and twenty-five business men on Main, Burdick and Rose streets, protesting against the proposed location of Water Works on Eleanor street, was presented to the Board.

The motion to locate said works on said lot, passed May 24th, was reconsidered and so amended as to locate the Water Works on DeKam's lot, near Axtell creek, on the east side of South Burdick street. (present location.)

Committee on Fire and Water instructed to negotiate for the purchase of the DeKam lot.

Lot on Eleanor street ordered to be sold.

'69—June 7. Water bonds to the amount of three thousand five hundred dollars, ordered to be issued to Anthony DeKam to pay for his lot, on South Burdick street, bought by the Village.

Committee on Fire and Water ordered to correspond with Holly Manufacturing Company and ascertain the price of engine and pumping machinery of a capacity double that now contracted for.

'69—June 10. Committee reported that engine and pumps, as proposed, would cost $25,000.

Trustee Phelps ordered to go to Lockport and make further inquiry into the cost of machinery of greater capacity.

'69—June 14. Trustee Phelps reported that the Holly Company refused to make lower prices for works of the proposed increased capacity.

Building large enough to contain the largest proposed Water Works, ordered to be built on the South Burdick street lot.

Finance Committee and Committee on Fire and Water ordered to accurately estimate and report the cost of the proposed enlargement of the Water Works.

Special election, to vote on the issue of $25,000 additional Water Bonds, was ordered for the 24th inst.

'69—June 19. Joint committee to estimate cost of enlargement of Water Works reported, by a printed circular, which had been distributed through the Village.

'69—June 24. Additional Water Works Bonds, to the amount of $25,000, were authorized by special election.

'69—July 20. Order made to pay Wm. Smith, of Pittsburg, on contract for pipe, $5,000.

Finance Committee ordered to prepare and issue additional bonds for $25,000.

Hon. T. T. Flagler, President of the Holly Manufacturing Company, being present, a contract between the Village and said Company, for enlarged engines and pumping machinery, was made and signed—the cost of the same to be $25,000; and an order was drawn in favor of said company, for the sum of

$10,000. [By arrangement with the Holly Company, the first contract for engines and machinery was surrendered to the Village, the company agreeing to keep the machinery first contracted for, on condition, that the Village pay $10,000 at once on the second contract for enlarged machinery.] Pipe laying commenced.

'69—Aug. 2. Committee on Fire and Water instructed to cover the roof of Water Works building with tin.

'69—Aug. 23. Fourteen hundred and forty-four dollars paid to Holly Company on contract, for machinery; and $5,000 to Wm. Smith for pipe.

'69—Sept. 6. Board ordered the payment of $6,250 to Holly Company on contract for machinery.

'69—Oct. 4. Order was made to pay $3,000 to Wm. Smith on pipe contract.

Trustee Phelps authorized to receive propositions from engineers, to take charge of the Water Works.

'69—Oct. 11. Committee on Fire and Water, together with Trustees Bishop and Cobb, appointed a special committee to frame a schedule of prices for the use of water.

'69—Oct. 15. Report of the special committee on Water Rates, was presented, amended and adopted.

Trustee Phelps appointed Superintendent of Water Works.

Chas. Barrett appointed engineer on a salary of $800 per annum and use of dwelling house on Water Works lot.

'69—Oct. 25. Engines started at midnight. After forcing the air out of the water mains, and raising the water pressure to 20 pounds to the square inch, it was found that the pipes were leaking in several places, especially at the corner of Burdick and Water streets, where a "cross" had been put in and one side stopped with a wooden plug. This plug was forced out causing a large hole in the street. Most of the leaks, however, were in the old piping that had been used for conducting water to the old cisterns, on Main street. Aside from this, no trouble was experienced.

'69—Nov. 1. Trustee Phelps reported that pipe, for Water Works is all received and laid, and that the Works will be ready for the decisive test on the 3th inst.

On motion, it was ordered, that Saturday, November 6th, be the day fixed for testing the Water Works, to determine whether or not they fulfill the conditions of the contract made by the Holly Company with the Village.

The Clerk of the Village was ordered to give notice, in the Village papers, of the day of trial.

A special committee of citizens, consisting of Hon. Chas. E. Stuart, John Dudgeon, Jonathan Parsons, Gilbert Wilson, J. W. Breese, Henry Gale, J. B. Cornell, L. H. Trask, J. A. B. Stone, D. D., H. G. Wells, J. Lomax, Henry Gilbert, Dr. E. H. VanDeusen, Dr. Foster Pratt, Dr. L. C. Chapin, S. S. Cobb, Ransom Gardner, Israel Kellogg and Alexander Cameron, was appointed and authorized to examine the contract made with the Village by the Holly Company, to witness the test to be made on the 6th inst., and to report whether, in their judgment, the test conditions of said contract are properly fulfilled; said committee was requested to meet the Village Board, in the Trustees room, Corporation Hall, on the 6th inst., at 1:30 P. M.

An order was made to pay Wm. Smith $3,500 on pipe contract.

'69—Nov. 6. Citizens' committee on test were authorized to add to their number, such mechanics and engineers, to aid in the examination and working of the machinery, as it may see fit.

Thos. O'Neill, Chief Engineer of the Fire Department, with twelve firemen to be detailed by him, were requested to assist in a further test of the Water Works to be made on Monday, Nov. 8th.

The Citizens' Committee met pursuant to call, at Corporation Hall, on Saturday, Nov. 6th, at 1:30 P. M., and organized by electing J. W. Breese, Chairman and Dr. Pratt, Secretary. The contract of the Holly Company with the Village was read to the committee, Hon. T. T. Flagler, President of the Company, being present. For convenience of action, the general committee appointed, from its own members, a sub-committee of seven, consisting of Dr. Foster Pratt, H. G. Wells, L. H. Trask, G. Wilson, J. A. B. Stone, J. Lomax, and J. W. Breese, instructing said sub-committee to embody in a report to the Village Board, the results of the general committee's observations during the test.

The first contract test, "to throw six one inch streams 100 feet high," was made on Main street, fifty feet of hose being attached to each hydrant located as follows: Corner of Main and Portage streets, one at the corner of Main and Burdick streets, one at the corner of Main and Rose streets, one at the corner of Main and Park streets, one in front of the residence of J. W. Breese on Main street, and one at the corner of Main and West streets. This test was well sustained even during a heavy wind from the south-west. Shortly after 2 o'clock P. M. a heavy, driving snow storm compelled the discontinuance, for the time, of the public test. But the machinery at the Water Works building was carefully examined and (the storm continuing) further tests were adjourned to Monday, Nov. 8th.

Messrs. P. Hobbs, Geo. Dodge, J. Brown, and Thos. Clarage, machinists and engineers, were added to the general committee and requested to examine the machinery and make a special report of the result of their observations, to the general committee.

'69—Nov. 8. Test resumed at 1 P. M. From the hydrant at the corner of Cedar and West streets water was thrown "through 1,000 feet of hose, from 70 to 80 feet high;" and "through 1,500 feet of hose" with nearly as favorable results. From the double hydrant, at the corner of Lovell and Rose streets, water was thrown ten feet above the top of the Methodist church tower— or 185 feet from the level of the street. The test of "six one inch streams 100 feet high" was repeated with complete success.

The committee met at Corporation Hall in the evening, and heard from Messrs. Hobbs and Dodge, on behalf of the mechanical committee, that their examination had been thorough and its results were satisfactory.

A vote was then taken in the general committee, on the several contract tests and each was unanimously sustained; after which the following resolution was unanimously adopted:

"RESOLVED, That the tests of the machinery for Water Works, provided in the contract between the Holly Manufacturing Company and the Village of Kalamazoo, have been fully and satisfactorily made, and that we hereby recommend the acceptance of said machinery. "

At a meeting of the Village Board, held the same evening, the report of the general committee (of which the foregoing is an abstract,) was presented and read to the President and Trustees by Dr. Pratt, chairman of the sub-committee, and, after discussion, it was adopted by the Board.

It was then ordered, by the Board, that $6,289.65 be paid to the Holly Company on account.

INTERMEDIATE AND INTRODUCTORY.

With the completion and acceptance of the Water Works we close the first general chapter of the history of Fire and Water in Kalamazoo.

Mistaken notions, more or less prevalent among our people, relative to the cost and economical value of our Water Works, make it proper, at this point, to indicate and discuss briefly, the true relations of these works to municipal economy, and the individual tax payer.

During all the first period of our municipal history (prior to Water Works,) water supply, though a necessary adjunct of a fire department, was, in all other respects, a matter of no moment or importance. But, from this time on, the Water Works, though, in one sense, a separate and important factor in municipal comfort and health, in another sense, and by their very principles of construction, became an integral and indivisible part of our fire department. Neither the Water Works nor the Fire Department can now be fully considered apart from the other. Formerly, the fire department, with a little water, put out fire; now, the Water Works, with a little lepartment, does the same, but does it more certainly and more efficiently than before. This statement of the relative rank and importance of the two fire agencies, no more implies depreciation of the human agency, than to say, that a locomotive, with an engineer, draws the train. The Water Works, therefore, perform the double function of furnishing a domestic water supply and a fire department.

The importance of a suitable water supply, for domestic, sanitary and mechanical purposes, seems to make many people forget, that this was not, and is not, their chief end and purpose; they forget that the works were designed and built, primarily and mainly, for fire protection. The very principles, on which they are constructed, demonstrate that they are more a fire engine than a pumping engine. By their nature, they are an efficient and economical fire department; but they are not, and they cannot be, the most economical agent of water supply alone. But, situated as we are, with regard to quantity and quality and sources of water supply, our two-fold wants and purposes are, probably, better and more economically served than they can be by any other arrangement possible to us.

It should not be overlooked or forgotten, that the Kalamazoo river, Portage, Arcadia, and Axtell creeks, Loring's lake and Allcott's spring, each and all in turn, have been repeatedly discussed as a source of water supply and that each and all, after investigation, have been as often dismissed from serious consideration, because of some insuperable objection.   To illustrate:

ALLCOTT's SPRING furnishes (according to Mr. Chesborough, of Chicago,) only 894,000 gallons of water in twenty-four hours.   This is not half enough, even for our present occasional necessities.

LORING's LAKE, nearly three and a-half miles southwest from the center of the village, furnishes, (according to the same authority) a little over 1,000,000 gallons in twenty-four hours: we frequently use, even now, a million and a-half, (1,500,000) gallons in the same time.

ARCADIA AND AXTELL CREEKS are also insufficient; but, even if their volume were enough for our present and prospective wants, their waters are manifestly impure and not fit to use.

PORTAGE CREEK OR THE KALAMAZOO RIVER furnish water enough, it is true; but their water, (for various reasons that need not now be enumerated or discussed, is not wholesome nor fit to drink.

A large WELL, therefore, such as we now have at the Water Works, and such, too, as may hereafter be constructed, either there or at some other suitable and convenient point, is the *only possible source*, from which Kalamazoo can draw a supply of water that is both pure and plenty.   And it was this fact that wisely guided the action of some who were most influential in locating the present Water Works and in determining the character or principles of the machinery to be used.

But, (it is objected) the works have cost too much.   This is true; but who knows of a young town, beginning a great municipal enterprise, that did not make mistakes—costly mistakes—that required subsequent and costly remedy?   Can those, who make this objection, be sure that there would have been no costly mistakes on some other plan?

It is further objected, that the running expenses of the Water Works are too great—that some other machinery, constructed on a different principle, could be operated more cheaply.   It has been already admitted, that other machinery, operating on a different principle, would furnish water, for daily supply, at less expense; but, (and this is the point constantly ignored by this class of objectors,) such machinery, as would furnish a large volume of water, at a low pressure, and at the least cost, *will not serve as a fire engine*; by changing the principle of our machinery, to cheapen the cost of domestic supply, we make steam fire engines and their costly concomitants necessary to the protection of our property from fire.

Now what are the facts? The running expenses of the Water Works, during the last fiscal year, was $6,857.71. The revenue and other credits, to which they are entitled, amount to $5,422.89; which leaves a balance, against the works, to be paid by the village, of $1,-434.82. This *seems* to show that they do not pay running expenses. But this is not all that can be said, and that must be said, if we mean to consider this question fairly and fully and justly.

The rates, to water users, are, in some respects, too low; and because of a useless waste, too much water is pumped. During the last year, the water pumped amounted to the enormous total (for a town of our size) of nearly 300,000,000 gallons. At the low rate of *three cents*, per thousand gallons, this amount of water pumped would give a revenue, for the year, of $9,000—or $2,500 in excess of running expenses. This is enough to demonstrate, that, by proper use of the water, the works can be made to pay their expenses.

Nor is this all; our Water Works, when economically considered, are entitled to large annual credits which they seldom, almost never, get. They do not get it, because it cannot be definitely stated in dollars and cents—it must be estimated. But for our Water Works, we would be compelled to maintain a costly steam fire engine department; and whatever is thus *saved*, by our works, to the Village and its tax payers, is a legitimate credit to the works.

Some of our sister towns, with a population equal to our's, have Water Works that furnish water, only for general use; steam fire engines and a fire department sufficient to man and to manage them, are, to such towns, a necessity. In such towns the expense of such a fire department uniformly reaches the large sum of $12,000 to $15,-000 a year. Our own fire department cost us, last year, $4,311.67. This difference, in our favor, of eight or ten thousand dollars per annum, cannot be credited to anything but our Water Works. Why, then, when we discuss among ourselves, the economical value of our works, do we so persistently neglect or refuse to credit them with the expense they *save* us? Let us credit them, therefore, in

our judgments, if not on our corporation books, with both the revenue they bring and the expense they save.

If, (as in some cities that use the Holly system,) our Water
Works were owned by a private corporation, we would soon find, *as
they do*, that our works are entitled to credit for *fire purposes*. If
we paid to a company, *as they do*, from forty to fifty dollars a year
for each hydrant, we would begin to realize the precise money value of *our* hydrants. We have 150 of them; at fifty dollars each, per
annum, we would find our own Water Works entitled to an annual
credit of $7,500, which they do not now get, simply because we do
not pay it. And yet, grumbling tax payers complain, because our
works are not self-sustaining. Give them due credits, gentlemen,
and they will give us fair dividends.

Speaking of dividends—who, even among our grumblers, would
give up the pure, bright, cool and sparkling water we drink—who
would forego the pleasure of seeing graceful fountains, green lawns
and beautiful flowers—who would willingly sacrifice the feeling of
security, from great and devastating fires, in which we all so comfort-
ably rest? Who, in short, to save a paltry tax, would consent to re-
mand Kalamazoo back to bad water, dusty streets, burnt lawns and
dangerous fires? These things may not be dollars and cents, but
are they not dividends? Indeed, when we come to sell our property,
do we not reckon them as dollars and cents? People of taste, who
come to live among us, are very sure to give them a money value,
when they buy a home.

"But," complains another, "they wear out and something must
be done to them every year—they are a constant bill of expense."
Yes, sir. Your boy wears out his clothes and must have new ones—
he grows bigger and must have bigger ones; do you complain of
that? If we had steam fire engines would they last forever? The
boilers and engines in your shops, that rest and cool, nights and Sun-
days, wear out; do you expect the machinery, at the Water Works
that never rests, day nor night, never to wear out? Do you expect
pumps and engines big enough for 8,000 people to be big enough for
12,000 people? Let us be reasonable—even while we pay taxes.

Twelve years ago the Water Works were built. Their operation
has improved the health and lessened the death rate of our people;
it has beautified our homes; it has lessened the damage from fire; it
has, in fact, lessened our taxes and increased the value of property

and the volume and the profit of our business.   The inauguration of our Water Works was a red letter day in our municipal history.

Having chronicled the events that precede it, let us now trace the subsequent history of our fire and water interests down to the present.

CHRONICLES–CHAPTER II.

1869—Nov. 29.   Chief Engineer of Fire Department, Thos. O'Neill, submitted a report recommending a reorganization of the Department to adapt it to the new conditions and wants created by the Water Works.   A plan of reorganization accompanied the recommendation, proposing that the department consist of four hose companies of twenty men each, which was referred to the Committee on Fire and Water.

Trustees Cobb and Bishop, with the Clerk, were appointed a committee to draft an ordinance for the reorganization and government of the Fire Department.

Messrs. J. Cornell, G. H. Gale, S. S. Cobb, and Thos. O'Neill were appointed a committee of citizens to confer with the Committee on Fire and Water, in respect to reorganization of the Fire Department.

'69—Dec. 6.   The foregoing committee reported in favor of the plan proposed by Mr. O'Neill, which was accepted and adopted.

'69—Dec. 9.   The roof of the Water Works building having taken fire from the smoke-pipe, the Board ordered 150 feet of hose and a ladder to be used at that building.

Negotiations with the Holly Co. for a " surface condenser " for the Water Works, were ordered.

Repairs ordered to Water Works building.

1870—Jan. 17.   The Committee on Fire and Water was instructed to report which of the old fire engines can best be sold.

'70—March 7.   Order made to pay Wm. Smith $1,400.11, in full for pipe.

The re-election of Thos. O'Neill, as Chief Engineer of the Fire Department, was confirmed.

Committee, to draft and report ordinance for the reorganization and government of the Fire Department, made a report which was adopted.   [Four Hose Companies of fifteen men each; including Foreman, Asst. Foreman, two Hydrantmen, and not less than two Pipemen. Each company to choose its own officers. Each Foreman to keep record of the time each man of his company is on duty. Fifteen citizens to be special "Fire Police," the President of the Village to be Chief thereof. A Chief and Asst. Chief Engineer.]

'70—MARCH 16.   Trustees Metcalf, Baumann and Bishop, ap-pointed a committee to consider and report the details of a more complete organization of the Fire Department.

'70—MARCH 19.   This committee reported in favor of one four wheeled Horse Hose Cart, to carry 1,200 to 1,500 feet of hose, and one two wheeled Horse Hose Cart, both to be kept at Cor-poration Hall and manned by twenty-five men; the company to be paid annually $400. That hose carts and Volunteer Compa-nies be located: one on or near West Street, between Main and Cedar Streets; one on or near Rose Street, between Vine and Dutton Streets; and one on Burdick Street, near M. C. R. R. Depot. Old Fire Engine, No. 2, to be located, over Portage, near Merrill & McCourtie's Mill.

'70—APRIL 11.   Charter election. Allen Potter, President; James H. Carr, Wm. G. Dewing, N. DeMary and L. C. Chapin, Trus-tees; Henry Bishop, J. C. Bassett, C. M. Hobbs and A. T. Met-calf hold over. Committee on Fire and Water, for ensuing year, C. M. Hobbs, Jas. H. Carr and A. T. Metcalf.

'70—APRIL 21.—Chief Engineer presented the resignations of the several Hose Companies, tendering therewith their services, in case of fire, until a permanent organization can be effected.

Vote of thanks, by Board, to Fire Department, for their "generous offer."

'70—MAY 16.   The old hand fire engines, on hand, were reported to be worth, respectively, as follows: No. 1, $1,200; No. 2, $700; No. 3, $300.

Charles B. Barrett and Geo. Storey, elected Engineer and Asst. Engineer, at Water Works, for the ensuing year, with $1,350 and house rent, for their joint services.

'70—MAY 20.   President Potter and Trustees Metcalf and Hobbs made a special committee to draft and report a plan of organ-ization of Fire Department.

Building belonging to Horace Phelps, on Lovell street,
and one belonging to John Dudgeon, on Burdick street, ordered
to be put in proper condition for Hose Carts and Companies.

'70—MAY 28.   Excelsior Hose Co., No. 2, consisting of 18 men,
to occupy Hose House on Lovell street, tendered its services,
which was accepted with thanks.   ·

'70—JUNE 6.   Numerous and pressing demands for the extension
of water pipes being made; it was ordered, that the issue of
$25,000 additional bonds be submitted to a special election to
be held June 18.

'70—JUNE 11.   Hose Co. No. 1, G. H. Gale, Foreman, consisting
of 27 men, and Hose Co. No. 3, C. M. Hobbs, Foreman, consisting of 29 men, severally tendered their services and were accepted.

'70—JUNE 18.   Additional Water Bonds, to the amount of $25,-
000, were voted at special election.

'70—JUNE 20.   Survey of the Village with regard to the proper
distribution of water pipes, and the purchase of $8,000 worth of
pipe and 25 double hydrants ordered.

'70—JULY 5.   A Rotary Engine and furnace chimney ordered for
Water Works.   Twenty more double hydrants ordered.

'70—JULY 22   Water pipe, of various sizes, to lay 23,000 feet,
was ordered to be put down on the several streets, and portions
of streets recommended by the Committee on Fire and Water.
Horse Hose Cart, not to cost more than $350, was ordered.

'70—SEPT. 25.   Committee on Fire and Water instructed to ar-
range for the care of the town clock and the fire alarm, at a cost
not to exceed $50 per annum.

'70—Nov. 7.   Oct. 18th, the Medical Association of Kalamazoo,
passed, unanimously, a resolution declaring "that the water of
Axtell creek cannot be used for culinary and drinking purposes
without danger to the Public Health."

Trustees Bishop and Dewing were appointed a committee
to confer with the Medical Association.

Lot, at Water Works, extended, on the south, by purchase of a lot costing $150, and the Committee on Fire and
Water ordered to straighten the creek.

Horse and harness, to cost not to exceed $250, for hose cart at Corporation Hall, was ordered.

Hand engine No. 1 (old "Burr Oak,") ordered sold.

'70—DEC. 5. Committee on Fire and Water authorized to hire two capable men to man Horse Hose Cart, at a cost, for both, not exceeding $60 per month. [This is the first step taken toward a paid fire Department.]

1871—FEB. 6 Committee on Fire and Water report cost of work and material for extending Water Works, during the year, $25,776.20, also,

Amount of water rates collected and due $1,600.●

'71—MARCH 6th. Thos. O'Neill's election as Chief Engineer of Fire Department confirmed.

'71—APRIL 10th. Election of Village officers. Dr. Foster Pratt, President; John K. Ward, A. M. Waterbury, Wm. R. Coats and John Beggs, Trustees. Holding over: L. C. Chapin, Wm. G. Dewing, J. H. Carr and N. Demary. Committee on Fire and Water consisted of Wm. R. Coats, A. M. Waterbury and J. H. Carr.

'71—APRIL 12th. Chief Engineer O'Neill reported proposition, from Fort Smith, Arkansas, to buy hand engine No. 1 ("Burr Oak") for $900. Ordered to be sold.   .

'71—APRIL 27th. President Pratt reported the north rotary pump at Water Works to be broken, and sent to Lockport for repairs.

The repairing and cleaning, regulating and winding of town clock and fire alarm referred to Trustee Coats with power to act.

'71—JUNE 5. Chief Engineer O'Neill made complaint that Engineer Barrett, at the Water Works, had refused to obey his orders in regard to speed and power of engine. Referred.

'71—JUNE 19. Rank and salaries of the two engineers at the Water Works made equal—the salaries to be $800 per annum.

Committee on Fire and Water, (reporting on the complaint made June 5th, by Chief O'Neill) informed the Board—that on the 5th inst., during a public display, the water in the "old well" had given out—that Engineer Barrett disclaimed any intentional disobedience of orders of the Chief Engineer of the Fire Department, and that he had done all, in his power, to make the firemen's display a success.

Chairman of the Committee on Fire and Water was authorized to make "certain repairs and improvements at the Water Works." [The improvements, here alluded to, consisted, mainly, in digging down the hill north of the Water Works and using the material to fill up and cover up the marshy ground south of the Water Works to the creek, as now straightened.]

'71—JUNE 26.   Ordered that the two remaining hand fire engines be put in good order and advertised for sale.

'71—JULY 17.   On motion of Trustee Chapin, the Chairman of the Committee on Fire and Water was authorized to sink an experimental pipe, four inches in diameter, at the proposed site for a new well.

[This order is the first official action of the Board contemplating a new well; and as the order itself, involves a geological question, that question, and its relation to the well can now be conveniently discussed.]

THE WELL
—AND—
ITS GEOLOGICAL RELATIONS.

Though, for nearly ten years, Kalamazoo has drawn abundance of pure and wholesome water, from the well at the Water Works, the origin or source of this unfailing water, seems to be, even yet, a puzzle to many, if not to most of our people. Of those who undertake to explain how the water is furnished, few succeed in demonstrating their possession of full knowledge of the subject. It is thought, therefore, not inappropriate to give, with this bit of local history, such an explanation, of the source and nature of our water supply, as will dispel at least the mystery in which, to some, it seems to be shrouded.

First—Negatively—The water in the well does *not* come from a "spring;" it does *not* flow from a "vein;" it does *not* percolate from "Axtell creek," nor from any other stream; nor is it, in any sense or degree, an "Artesian Well."

Second—Its success, as a source of water supply, is due solely to the peculiar and rare geological conditions which characterize this portion of the Kalamazoo valley. These geological conditions, though relatively rare, are simple; and, with the geological clew, it is easy to understand *how* the water supply is furnished and *why* it is abundant and good.

The outcroppings of stratified rock, (on the north at Grand Rapids with a dip to the south, on the east at Jackson with a dip to the west, on the south in Branch and Hillsdale counties with a dip to the north, and on the west at several points with a dip to the east) all indicate, that where Kalamazoo valley now is, there was formed in some past age, a great rocky bowl or basin. This basin (an arm or part of the Lake Michigan basin) seems to have been about one hundred and fifty miles long, by about one hundred miles wide; and the rock bottom of the bowl also seems to have been (and yet to be) some 500 to 700 feet below what is now the surface of the ground.

At sometime, in the far off past, this basin must have been filled by "drift"—such as boulders, gravel, sand with some clay and mud— which was brought and left here, partly, during what is called a "glacier period," and partly during the "pliocene period," during both of which periods, (according to Agassiz and other geological authorities) the Atlantic basin extended from Baffin's Bay and Davis' Strait on the northeast, down through Hudson's Bay, the basin of our great lakes, and the Mississippi valley, to the Gulf of Mexico. (The abundance and peculiar character, of the ocean products, yet found in our soil, not to speak of other evidences, strongly support this theory of the great geologists.)

During some subsequent age, Michigan and a portion of British territory north of us, were raised, by volcanic upheaval, so as to form three great water sheds; one. from Hudson's Bay by way of Davis' Strait; one, by way of the St. Lawrence; and one, by the Mississippi river. This general upheaval seems to have detached the present Kalamazoo basin from its connection with the Lake basin, except as its waters are drained by the Kalamazoo river into the Lake. As the waters drained off, because of this uplifting of our locality, Michigan was left with her surface shaped, substantially, as we now see it.

But these geological theories, whether true or untrue, are not important to this discussion, except so far as they rationally account for the general geological *facts* which remain and are now apparent. The important and essential fact is this: That beneath us we find *water intermingled with porous material,* (such as sand, gravel and boulders,) to an indefinite depth. A boring, (the deepest we know of) made at the Spring Works, on Portage street, by Mr. Egleston, to the depth of about one hundred and forty feet, develops no stratified rock, but demonstrates, that water and "drift" are intermingled all the way down.

This intermingling of water with "drift," and its effects on the movements of the water therein, may be illustrated, by supposing a large bowl or dish half full of water, to be filled with gravel until the water is entirely covered and disappears from sight. It is plain, in this supposed case: first, that water will be found at the *same level*, everywhere in the dish; second, that, at all points, below the surface of the water level, the water will fill equally and uniformly all the interstices between the gravel; and third, that if by pumping up through a small tube, the water level be lowered at any point, the other water, obeying hydraulic law, will flow rapidly, through the gravel, towards the lowered point of the water surface.

This represents the essential, if not the exact, conditions found in the rocky basin we call the Kalamazoo valley. This basin of rock, (one hundred and fifty miles long by one hundred miles wide, the bottom of which is several hundred feet below the present surface of the ground,) was once full of water; sand, gravel, boulders, etc., have been dropped from floating icebergs, or drifted by water currents into this basin, displacing an equal bulk of water, and filling it so full as to cover the water out of sight, and to make dry land; but, in this big bowl, as in the little one, we find water, with essential regularity, at a certain water level. Our private wells, dug for water, are of different depths because of the elevations and depressions of the ground surface, but they all reach water, substantially, at the same water level. (There are some exceptions to this rule, in wells on our hillsides, caused by accidental strata of clay; but they need not be discussed; they are exceptions to the otherwise general rule.) Thus, at the foot of Main street, a well may be fifteen feet deep; at the Kalamazoo House twenty feet; at the corner of Main and West streets twenty-eight feet; at the foot of Prospect Hill thirty-five feet; and on Grand Prairie from 120 to 150 feet deep, and yet all find water *at the same level* and in *the same kind of material.*

The well at the Water Works and all our private wells operate, therefore, in all respects, upon the *same principles*, the differences between them consisting, solely, in diameter and depth. While the private well, three feet in diameter, goes four feet into the water stratum, the well, at the Water Works, twenty-four feet in diameter, is sunk twenty-six feet into the same water stratum.

The accompanying diagram, of a perpendicular section of our valley from east to west, illustrates, rudely but fairly, all these facts:

the rock supposed to constitute the basin; the intermingling of water with sand and gravel in the basin; the undulations of the land surface, which is the reason why our private wells differ in depth; the bed of the Kalamazoo river which drains off the overplus of water from rain and snow; the fact that the well, at the Water Works, is just like our other wells, (except that it is bigger and deeper); and makes plain the fact, that the water supply, *to* the well being unlimited, the supply *from* it is also unlimited, except as retarded, in its flow toward the well, by the loose material intermingling with it. It also shows that, when the well is lowered, by pumping at the Water Works, below the general level of the water stratum, a "head" is thereby created, in the water outside of the well, by which water is forced into the well, at its bottom, with a force and rapidity exactly proportioned to the lowering of the well.

The question is often asked: "If our private wells are rendered impure by the percolation of sewage through a porous soil down to the water stratum, why is not the water of the public well, just as impure?" This is a pertinent and important question which requires a full and explicit answer.

There are two reasons for the difference: First, The water, in private wells, comes from the *surface* of the water stratum, which first receives the sewage pollution; while the water, supplying the large well, comes from a point twenty-six feet below the *surface* of the water stratum, and thirteen feet below the *bottom* of the river and of all the other streams that drain the basin. For these reasons the water from the works can be but little, if at all, polluted by the cause that poisons our old private wells.

Second—But this is not the only nor is it the principal reason for the difference in the qualities of the two kinds of well water. The great well curb, when sunk, passed through a stratum of clay impervious by water and some four feet in thickness, which extends beneath the village, thereby separating the upper from the lower water. This stratum is found, as a rule, some six to eight feet below the water surface, and four or five feet below the bottoms of our average private wells. Over this clay bed, therefore, percolates the polluted upper water to the Kalamazoo river and the other streams that drain the basin. This is the main and real protection of the purity of the lower water furnished to and by the well.

Further—Whatever the cause of it may be, the water from the works is shown to be pure, *in fact*, by careful and skillful analysis made

at different times—before the well was sunk; immediately after the
water began to be used; and at intervals, of a year or two, ever since
and it has always been found to be free from all forms of organic matter.   No amount of organic matter capable of being weighed—only
"a trace"—has ever been found by expert analytical chemists, in frequently repeated trials, during the ten years of its existence.   If this
water is ever to be polluted, as our private wells are, ten years of
constant and enormous draft, on its water resources should and would
have developed it.

Certain facts, having a geological basis, have been developed by
the construction and operation of our "big well," which should be
carefully noted.

First—That the water stratum, beneath us, if properly developed, furnishes a pure and abundant supply of water.

Second—That whenever the necessities of our growth and enterprises compel an increase of the water supply, it can be easily
and cheaply met by the construction of another well, in a proper location, to be connected with the one now in use.

Third—That those who, by location, cannot use the water from
the works and whose wells have become impure, may obtain the same
quality of water—just as good in all respects—as that furnished by
the big well.   This may be done by driving a "drive well" to a depth
not less than twenty or twenty-five feet below the *bottoms* of their
old wells.   By doing this they will draw water from the same source,
from the same level, and of the same quality as that furnished by the
Water Works.

'71—JULY 31. Committee on Fire and Water authorized to purchase lot next north and adjoining the Water Works at a cost
not exceeding $1,100.

'71—AUG. 29. Trustees Chapin and Ward, Special Committee, authorized to visit La Porte, Ind., and examine the operations of
Holly's "Gang Pump" in use by the Water Works of that city.

'71—SEPT. 9. Chairman Coats, of the Committee on Fire and Water, reported plans and specifications for improving and increasing the supply of water at the Water Works, by the construction of a new and larger well. Adopted, by yeas and nays, as
follows:

Yeas—Trustees Carr, Chapin, Coats, Dewing, Waterbury,
and the President—6.

Nays—Trustee Demary—1.

By resolution, the Chairman of the Committee on Fire and Water was authorized and instructed to proceed forthwith to the construction of the proposed new well.

1872—MARCH 4. Resolutions of thanks to the authorities, firemen and citizens of Kalamazoo, passed by the Common Council of Grand Rapids, Feb'y. 24th, 1872, for their prompt response to a call for help on the night of the burning of Sweet's Hotel—received and filed.

'72—MARCH 11. Horse for hose cart, reported disabled and sale authorized.

Special Committee reported an ordinance, establishing a Board of Water Commissioners, which was adopted.

'72—MARCH 18. Committee on Fire and Water made a special report of a test of the capacity of the new well made on the 16th inst. and recommending a public test under the direction of a large committee of citizens.

Accordingly, a Citizens Committee, numbering sixty, was appointed and requested to meet on Wednesday, March 25th, at Corporation Hall, at 2 P. M., for the purpose of conducting a public test of the capacity of the new well.

Thos. O'Neill was requested to assist at the test and to detail, from the fire department, a sufficient number of men to render all needed aid to the committee.

'72—MARCH 25. The committee of sixty, appointed to conduct the test of the capacity of the new well to furnish water, reported, through its chairman, Gen. Dwight May:

"That 'the well' is a perfect success. In our judgment, it may be considered a FIXED FACT, that we now have an abundant supply, of pure water, for all purposes."

[The report of the general committee enclosed the special reports of four sub-committees—one, on source of water supply; one, on the rapidity of pumping; one, on the effect of pumping on the water level in the well; and one on the number of streams used and of hydrants opened. See village daily papers, of March 26th, 1873.]

The President was appointed a special committee to collate and prepare a report of the same for publication.

The Committee, on Fire and Water, was authorized to construct a covering or dome over the new well, according to plans and specifications presented by its chairman.

[The well being now finished, tested and appproved, the mode of its construction is in order.]

THE WELL.
—AND—
HOW IT WAS CONSTRUCTED.

The most important event in the history of the Kalamazoo Water Works, was the discovery, and development of the present water supply.

This was begun in 1871 and was fully completed early in 1872.

Immediately after the organization of the Board of Trustees in April, 1871, the question of an improved water supply was brought before the Board in such a manner as to command attention, and action.

The health officer of the Village, H. O. Hitchcock, M. D., served a notice upon the Chairman of the Committee on Fire and Water, protesting against the use of the existing water supply, for domestic purposes.

Until this time it had been the general belief that the water in use was good, because it was supposed, that the water supply, was furnished by a spring discovered in sinking the original well.

The Chairman of the Committee on Fire and Water at once made an investigation, with the assistance of the health officer, and very soon established the fact that it was the Axtell brook, and not the aforesaid spring, that furnished the principal supply.

An analysis of this water conclusively proved that the health officer was justified in remonstrating against its further use for domestic purposes.

The chairman of the committee, as a temporary expedient, to improve the water as far as practicable, until some *permanent* plan could be determined upon, constructed a rude filter of gravel and sand, through which the brook water was passed before going to the pumps.

All who were officially interested, and many others, recognized the importance of better water, and many projects were canvassed, mainly looking to the removal of the pumping works, to a new source of supply, or bringing it from a distance to the pumping works.

Meanwhile the chairman of the committee was prosecuting a se-ries of experiments that finally resulted in the solution of the vexed question, by the development of the water now in use.

At this time nothing was known of the water stratum underlying the village of Kalamazoo, and the surrounding country, to any great-er depth than it is penetrated by the ordinary wells.

While it was generally known that the water stratum which supplied these ordinary wells was general, and found at an unusual-ly uniform level, nothing was known of the depth or nature of the deeper water.

Certain developments about this time, (during the summer of 1871) suggested the propriety of ascertaining the nature of the strata in which the first well was sunk.

Upon exhausting the water from said well, which was easily done after closing the conduit connecting the brook with the well, an examination of the material in which the well terminated, showed it to be a close, compact stratum of sand. A tube was sunk to a depth of twenty-two feet, in the bottom of this old well, developing the fact that this close, compact sand stratum referred to, extended to the depth of fourteen feet below the bottom of the well, or twenty-one feet below the surface level of the brook, at which point a coarse gravel stratum was reached, which gave evidence of carrying a large amount of water.

Quite a remarkable thing resulted from penetrating this open gravel stratum. *Water at once rose to the heighth of six feet above the level of the water in the brook.*

This furnished the key to the successful solution of the problem The well referred to reached the depth of seven feet below the brook level, and the water rising in the tube to the heighth of six feet above the brook level, gave for purposes of experiment a line of tubing ex-tending thirteen feet above the bottom of the well.

That portion of the tube above the bottom of the well was taken off, and replaced with one made in sections. A section was then re-moved from the upper end of the tube and the overflow timed and measured, then another section was removed and the process re-peated. The chairman of the committee and those officially inter-ested soon obtained sufficient. evidence to warrant the conclusion that an abundant supply of water could be obtained by cutting a proper opening through the overlying sand stratum to the open gravel beneath, and upon submitting the result of his experiments to the Board of Trustees, a majority of them agreed with him.

An analysis of this water was now made from samples taken from various depths, and it was found that the quality was all that could be desired after reaching a depth of twelve feet below its upper, or surface level.

The question of quality and quantity being settled, the question of development came next in order.

This was looked upon at the time (this being the pioneer work of the kind in this country) as almost a hopeless task.

The chairman of the committee, however, soon succeeded in perfecting plans upon which he was willing to *guarantee* success, and upon submitting his plans to the Board, they were adopted, and he was authorized to proceed with the work.

The plan in brief, was to construct a curb, or caison, twenty-four feet in diameter and about thirty feet in height, finishing it complete, and sinking it to place without removing any water from its interior.

This curb was built of iron and masonry, circular in form. The base upon which the masonry rested was of cast iron, with a lower cutting edge in order that the great weight of the structure should force the cutting edge downward as fast as the earth was removed from the interior.

The wall was 26 inches in thickness at the base with a batter on the outer side of six inches to the top, to lessen friction in sinking. It was impervious to water, and the whole supply was admitted at the bottom.

The work was accomplished successfully and reported finished and ready for the final test on March 18th, 1872.

A committee of sixty citizens was appointed by the Board to conduct the test.

It was made on the 25th day of March, 1872, and was in the highest degree satisfactory and successful, and our water supply has ever since been the pride of our village.

But few at that time had any faith in the success of the enterprise; but an incident will serve to show how firm was the faith of the chairman of the committee—Mr. Coats—in the final success of the work. As the test began he placed one thousand dollars in the hands of Col. F. W. Curtenius, of the citizens committee, telling him that if he could with all the pumping capacity of the works, reduce the level of the water in the well *six feet*, that he was at liberty to use the money to entertain the committee. It is sufficient to say, the committee did not use the money.

Our present supply is considered the best drinking water in the country. So clear and transparent is it that an object no larger than a five cent piece can be distinctly seen on the bottom of the well, through twenty-four feet of water.

'72—APRIL 1. Messrs. L. H. Trask, Alex. Buell, Thos. S. Cobb, Geo. H. Gale, Allen Potter, and Wm. G. Pattison, unanimously elected Water Commissioners, by the Village Board.

'72—APRIL 8. Village election held, electing Allen Potter, President; and C. S. Dayton, B. S. Williams, D. T. Allen, and Frank Henderson, Trustees.

'72—APRIL 10.—The President and Trustee Coats appointed a special committee to aid in the organization of the Board of Water Commissioners.

'72—APRIL 15. This committee reported that the Board of Water Commissioners was duly organized April 13, 1872.

By a communication from T. S. Cobb, Secretary of the Commissioners, the Village Board was informed that L. H. Trask had been elected President, and T. S. Cobb, Secretary, of the Board of Water Commissioners.

By resolution, unanimously adopted, the possession, management and operation of the Water Works were transferred from the Village Board to the said Board of Water Commissioners.

Committee on Fire and Water, for the ensuing year, W. R. Coats, D. T. Allen, and Frank Henderson.

'72—APRIL 17. A report was made by the Board of Water Commissioners in reference to the dangerous condition of one of the boilers at the Water Works. The Commissioners were authorized to purchase a new boiler, to replace the defective one reported on.

G. Henry Gale was recommended by the Board of Water Commissioners as Superintendent of the Kalamazoo Water Works; the recommendation was accepted and Mr. Gale appointed.

'72—MAY 6. An ordinance establishing water rates, together with rules and regulations governing the same was passed, and is known as Ordinance No. 18. The rates so established gave very general satisfaction to the citizens of the Village, and were very much lower than those of surrounding towns and cities.

'72—MAY 27. The Superintendent of the Water Works was authorized to purchase six water metres for use in such places as may be deemed advisable, to ascertain actually the consumption of water.

'72—JULY 1. A communication was received from the secretary of Eureka Hose Company No. 1, in which the company requested an appropriation of $500 to purchase uniforms.

The prayer of the Fire Boys was granted, and an appropriation made for such purpose, not to exceed the sum named in the communication.

[The action of the Board in the matter of this appropriation was reconsidered and then laid on the table.]

'72—AUG 7. Report made on new horizontal boiler at Water Works, it being now in position and proving entirely satisfactory: size of boiler, length 14 feet, diameter 6 feet, having 78 four inch tubes, the total cost including setting and extension of boiler room, $5,000.

'72—SEPT. 30. A recommendation was presented from the Board of Water Commissioners, advising the extension of water mains on West Main street, Kalamazoo avenue, and Stuart avenue. The whole matter was laid over for future consideration.

'72—OCT. 6. Mr. Graves was appointed Chief Engineer of the Water Works, and served as such for one year.

1873—JAN'Y. 6. At the regular meeting of the Board of Trustees, on motion of Trustee Ward, Luther H. Trask and Alexander Buell were elected Water Commissioner for the full term of three years.

A petition was received from the Board of Underwriters praying for relief from the extra hazard created by the continued construction of wooden buildings contiguous to business blocks on Main street.

The petition was laid over indefinitely.

'73—MARCH 3. In consequence of the failure of water supply at a recent large fire, which failure subjected the Chief Engineer of the Fire Department, the Superintendent and Engineers of the Water Works to blame, Mr. Gale addressed the Board on the subject, and requested the appointment of a special committee to investigate the cause of such failure. The following committee was appointed: Trustees Williams, Coats and Allen.

'73—MARCH 15. An extension of the fire limits to include blocks from Church street to Park street, north from Main street to Eleanor street was passed, and the same ordered printed.

'73—APRIL 7. The special committee appointed "to investigate the cause of failure of water supply for fire purposes" made the following report:

That, after various tests having been made and competent engineers consulted on the subject, the fact appeared conclusive that but two efficient fire streams could be obtained from the four inch mains at any point in the Village, and then only under a pressure such as to strain the present machinery to such an extent as to create great danger. The cause of this is mainly attributable to the wearing out of the "Holly Rotaries," it being simply impossible to keep up a supply at a moderate rate of speed in their present condition. The replacing of these pumps would obviate the difficulty, but only for a short time. The committee recommend a change of pumps at the earliest possible moment, as the only means to remove the danger permanently, and also recommend the size of the pumps to be greatly increased."

'73—APRIL 14. An order was made for the relaying of water mains below freezing depth on West Main street.

'73—MAY 5. An ordinance was passed repealing the by-law of the Village "for the establishment of a Board of Water Commissioners" enacted March 11th, 1872.

'73—MAY 12. The Committee on Fire and Water was instructed to erect a Fire Alarm Telegraph line from Corporation Hall to the Water Works, and to proceed with the work at once.

[Such line was erected and proved a valuable adjunct, not only as a convenience, but as an additional safety in the working of the department. Total cost, $684.00.]

U. O. Krause was appointed Superintendent of the Water Works at a salary of $1,000.00.

[Mr. Krause acted in such capacity till the spring of 1877.]

'73—JUNE 17.   At a special meeting of the Village Board a proposition was submitted by the Holly Manufacturing Company, of
Lockport, N. Y., for the furnishing of a pair of piston pumps;
the capacity of such to be 1,000,000 gallons in 24 hours; also a
proposition for a new boiler to replace the one reported unsafe.
The piston pumps to be furnished for the sum of $2,000.00.

'73—JUNE 18.   A contract was made with the Holly Manufacturing Company for one pair of piston pumps, capacity 1,000,000
gallons, and ratified by the Board.

'73—AUG. 4.   A request was submitted to the Board, praying for
the sinking of one or more artesian wells, and that the Board
authorize the same to be done and furnish means for the experiment.

No action was taken in the case.

[It is generally conceded it would need boring to the depth
of at least 600 feet before reaching a stratum that would insure
a self-flowing well.]

'73—AUG. 11.   Estimates to the amount of $10,000 were submit-
ted by the Committee on Fire and Water for the extension of
the water mains.

'73—OCT. 6.   The Committee on Fire and Water made report on
the new piston pumps:

"That they had been connected with the necessary machinery, and
the test made had been in every way satisfactory."

One feature of the test was the demonstration that the piston pumps were in every way better fitted for fire purposes than
the old rotaries; not needing the same rate of speed to be kept
up, and consequently not only safer but more economical.

On recommendation of the Chief Engineer of the Fire Department, the Superintendent of the Water Works and the
Foreman of each Hose Company were made Fire Wardens.

James Fox was appointed Chief Engineer of the Water
Works, and remained till June, 1874, giving general satisfaction in the discharge of his various duties.

'73—DEC. 1.   Reports were made of the general repairs at the
Water Works, viz:

"That a new No. 3 Knowles Pony Pump had been put in position at
a cost of $350.00, and the old Holly one removed as unsafe and not to be
depended on as a boiler feeder.   The engines had been changed to 'non-

condensing,' and thorough repairs had been made on lower parts of the building."

[It is the opinion of the present engineer and others who are competent to judge that a great mistake was made in changing to "non-condensing" engines.]

1874—MARCH 27. The Passenger Depot of the Grand Rapids and Indiana Railroad, on East Main street, was totally destroyed by fire. Cause of fire unknown. In consequence of the bursting of two hydrants the department were unable to save any of the Passenger House, but by their persevering efforts the surrounding property was saved from destruction.

'74—MAY 4. Ordinance No. 24, in relation to the construction of buildings within the fire-limits amended and the Committee on Fire and Water empowered under the same to pass upon the construction of buildings within said limits.

'74—JUNE 4. Geo. H. Chandler appointed Chief Engineer of the Water Works.

[Mr. Chandler still retains his position, and has by his continual energy and the faithful discharge of his duties, made himself very popular as Chief of the Kalamazoo Water Works.]

'74—JULY 6. Petition for the foundation of a Hose Company south and east of Portage Creek reported on favorably, and fifteen men recommended as a sufficient strength for same.

[This matter was subsequently reconsidered and reported on adversely.]

'74—AUG. 3. The Committee on Fire and Water were authorized to negotiate for the construction of a *New Boiler* at the Water Works, the cost not to exceed $1600.00.

'74—OCT. 9. A fire occurred at 5:30 A. M., totally destroying the building owned by Chase & Dewing, used as a Fanning Mill manufactory; two hundred feet of Rubber hose was lost in this fire, which in a great measure explains the destruction of so much property; no blame can attach to the Department, as they were compelled to lay long lines of hose in an alley and could not take them up in time to save them.

'74—NOV. 2. The Committee on Fire and Water made report in regard to the new boiler manufactured by Kimball & Austin M'f'g Co., for the Water Works, size of same being, diameter

5 feet, length 14 feet, with 78 3-inch tubes, and that they found the same to be sound and first-class in every particular. Total cost of boiler and setting, together with enlargement of building was $3,500.00. A special committee of three were appointed by President May, viz.: Trustees Sherwood, Dudgeon and Parker, to examine into the present and probable future condition and operation of the Water Works of the Village, and to report to the Board on the completion of their labors.

'74—DEC. 2. A disastrous fire occurred this evening on East Main street, totally destroying the Gates Morocco factory, consisting of three two story frame buildings. A great drawback in handling the fire was experienced in consequence of the main being only four inches; one fire stream was all it was possible to obtain. Loss estimated at $35,000; total insurance of $22,000. It required the utmost exertion of the Fire Department and volunteer aid from the citizens to save the adjoining property, and a great portion of the goods contained in the factory were also saved by volunteer aid.

1875—JAN'Y 4. The Committee on Fire and Water, through the Chairman, Mr. Dudgeon, made report in full of all water pipe, their sizes and location, also the number of fire hydrants in use. The report gives ten miles and 3,990 feet of all sizes of pipe as now laid, and 102 fire hydrants.

[For a full statement of all pipe, gates and hydrants, their location, etc., see tables " D," " E " and " F."

'75—FEB'Y 1. Under resolution of Trustee Sherwood, Mr. Frank Little as clerk of the Board, was instructed to furnish the special Committee on " Water Works" a tabular statement of expenditures for the Fire Department and Water Works during each of the four years last past, commencing with the organization of the Board of 1870.

[Such report was duly furnished to the committee by Mr. Little, and was incorporated by them in their report.]

'75—APRIL 19. The special Committee on Water Works was re-organized, the President appointed Trustees Wagner and Dayton to fill vacancies—the committee now being Messrs. Sherwood, Wagner and Dayton.

'75—MAY 29. A fire occurred at 3:45 A. M., consuming the Burdick House barn. Though surrounded by wooden buildings, the efforts of the Department were successful in preventing a spread of the conflagration to the business block contiguous to it. Loss about $1,500.

'75—JULY 9. A terrible fire occurred this morning at 4:15, destroying the Livery and Feed barn of Henry First, on Water street. Eleven horses were burned and a large amount of property destroyed. Six streams were used; it required the united exertion of all the members of the Fire Department to save the block of buildings on the north side of Main street, but the boys did not fail in the hour of need, and by their steady obedience to orders and fearless conduct throughout, saved the Village from a most calamitous loss. Estimated loss on property $3,500, on horses $3,000.

A fire alarm telegraph was established from the Michigan Central Railroad depot to Corporation Hall. Total cost of same $500.

The condenser at the Water Works was found so full of lime it could not be used with safety and the committee, under order of the Board, took it out and put in a Stillwell Heater and Lime Extractor, at a cost of $499.

'75—SEPT. 6. A complimentary resolution passed by the Common Council of Grand Rapids, thanking our Department for their tender of services at the late fire in Grand Rapids, was read and ordered placed on file.

'75—OCT. 27. The Kalamazoo Mastic Co's buildings burned this morning at 9:50, cause of fire unknown. Loss about $8,000. The fire when reached was under too great headway for the Department to save anything.

'75—NOV. 1. [Water pipe during the past season was ordered laid on quite a number of streets, but only a portion of such pipe was put in the ground.]

A hose house was ordered built in the southeast portion of the Village, over the Portage creek, not to exceed in cost $125.

1876—JAN'Y 3. The report of the special committee appointed Nov. 2, 1874, "to examine into the present and probable future condition and operation of the Water Works of the Village" was submitted by the chairman, T. R. Sherwood, which was accepted and ordered placed on file.

[This report, together with the tabular statement of expenditures furnished by Mr. Little was ordered printed with the annual report of the Board of Trustees for the year ending April, 1876.

'76—JAN'Y. 11.   A remonstrance of hose companies (against the injustice of asking services from such companies without any renumeration for such service) was submitted, and after considerable discussion, on motion the whole matter was indefinitely postponed.

Notice of the organization of a volunteer hose company south of Portage creek, with a list of officers and members was submitted to the Board stating "that the company tendered their service to the Village as firemen, and that their company was to be known as Victor Hose Company No. 4.   The organization was affirmed, the company accepted and ordered attached to the Fire Department of the Village, under the name and title as above stated.

'76—MARCH 13.   After considerable discussion with reference to the advisability of changing the volunteer fire department into that of a paid system, a resolution was passed accepting Eureka Hose Company No. 1, Vigilant Hose Company No. 3, and the Empire Hook and Ladder Company as reorganized.

[The details of the further organization of the fire department was left in the hands of the Committee on Fire and Water with power to act.]   Such companies, together with Victor Hose Company No. 4, to constitute the fire force of the village.

'76— AUG. 6.   Lyon & Page's warehouse burned at 12:45 A. M. Though a rag house and nearly full of stock, by the prompt action of the fire department, quite a large amount of property was saved.

'76—Nov. 14.   The Committee on Fire and Water made a report in regard to the condition of the Water Works pumps, "stating the rotary pumps to be entirely useless and the piston pumps now in use (constantly) as being entirely inadequate to supply sufficient water in case of a heavy fire and extremely unsafe, especially under a fire pressure.   The present capacity of the works is only 1,000,000 gallons in twenty-four hours.   The committee recommend the taking out the rotary pumps, their place to be supplied with two good piston pumps of the capacity of 2,000,000 gallons per day."

[The consideration of this subject occupied the attention of the Board for a number of months, during which time a great many propositions were submitted and thoroughly investigated, the committee and Board feeling the great importance of getting the best possible machinery and at the least expense consistent with thorough efficiency and safety.]

1877—FEB. 17. A further report of the Fire and Water Committee was submitted "recommending the purchase of a Worthington high pressure pumping engine, the capacity of such engine to be at least 2,000 000 gallons in twenty-four hours, and capable of sustaining a water pressure of 150 pounds to the square inch.

Under resolution of Trustee Hill the committee was authorized to purchase and place in the Water Works the above described Worthington pumping engine and to remove the Holly Rotary pumps now in position at the works, the total cost of such pumping engine of a capacity of 2,000,000 gallons in twenty-four hours, not to exceed the sum of $5,000, and a sufficient bond to be given by the manufacturers, to the village, guaranteeing the power, capacity and workmanship of such pumping engine to be according to specifications submitted, and that all pertaining to the machinery shall be entirely satisfactory to the Board.

'77—MARCH 16. Under resolution the purchase of the pumping engine for for the Water Works was postponed to the first regular meeting of the Board in May next.

'77—MAY 7. Contract authorized by new Board with H. R. Worthington, of New York for one high pressure duplex pumping engine, size and cost of same to be as stated in resolution passed February 17th, 1877.

Dimension of engine and pumps, two steam cylinders 29 inches inside diameter, $25\frac{1}{2}$ inch stroke, two water plungers 15 inches diameter and $25\frac{1}{2}$ inch stroke. [It has since been reported by the engineer in charge of works, the capacity is 2,000,000 gallons with a speed of 75 strokes per minute against a head of 250 feet.]

Chas. E Smith was appointed as Water Commissioner at a salary of $500 and by close supervision of this department increased the revenue considerably over that heretofore obtained by the Village.   [Mr. Smith served as Commissioner for two years.]

'77—May 23.   A reduction was made on water rates amounting to about 15 per cent.

'77—Oct. 27.   Contract authorized by the Board for lease of hose house on North Burdick street for the use of Vigilant Hose Company No. 3, at a rental of $150 per year.   [Lease was not signed till March 4, 1878.]   Trustee Dewing, Chairman of the Committee on Fire and Water presented a report, (after due consultation with his committee) recommending the dismissal from further service as firemen the hose company known as Eureka Hose Company No. 1, and the employment of three more regular paid firemen, besides those at present employed, the total paid men to act as firemen and policemen, and that all such men sleep at Corporation Hall.

The report was adopted and the Chairman of the Committee on Fire and Water, and Chairman of Committee on Police, together with the Chief Engineer of the Fire Department, authorized to select the proposed men for the Paid Fire Department: they were authorized to draft such rules and regulations as were necessary for the guidance of the employees of the department.

Under resolution, a force of six full paid men were to constitute the Paid Fire Department of the Village, and to be subject to and under the control of the Chief Engineer of the Fire Department, and that such company occupy a portion of Corporation Hall known as Eureka Hose Company division; the increase or decrease of such force shall be at the direction of the chairmen of the Committees on Fire and Water and Police, together with the Chief Engineer of the Fire Department. Rate of wages established at $35.00 per month, except captain, whose wages was made $40.00 per month.   Also, that all employees shall be subject to the rules and regulations of the Fire Department and the penalties thereunto attached.

The Chief Engineer of the Fire Department was instructed to tender to Eureka Hose Company the thanks of the Board for the valuable services the company had rendered the Village, and to notify them that their services as firemen would not be needed after the 31st day of the present month.

'77—Nov. 5. Trustee Dewing submitted the reports of Chief Engineer Chandler, of the Water Works, and Chiet O'Neill, of the Fire Department, giving the result of the recent test made of the Worthington Duplex Pumping Engine, made on the 26th and 28th days of September, 1877:

WATER WORKS, KALAMAZOO, Oct. 1, 1877.

W. S. Dewing, Esq., Chairman Fire and Water Committee, Kalamazoo Village:

DEAR SIR—I submit to your committee the following tests of the Worthington Duplex Pumping Engine just erected at the Water Works:

September 26th—Test in regard to capacity for ordinary domestic use; engine making 124 strokes per minute against a water pressure of 40 pounds, as shown on the guage, with 16½ feet suction, discharging at the rate of 3,784,320 gallons per 24 hours, lowering water in the WELL 8 feet 11½ inches; water discharged through open hydrants; engine working smoothly, with an average steam pressure of 47½ pounds.

September 28th—Test of engine for fire pressure. Duration of test forty-five minutes; wood consumed 1⅛ cords; average water pressure 133⅞ pounds; stroke per minute 88⅝; length of stroke 25½ inches; water pumped in 45 minutes 75,625 gallons; water in WELL lowered 5 feet 4 inches; lift of suction 12 feet 11 inches. After this test, pumping was done for four hours without any additional fuel, the engine making 24 strokes per minute under a water pressure of 40 pounds; making a total of 181,031 gallons pumped with 1⅛ cords of wood.

GEO. H. CHANDLER, Engineer.

[On the test of the 26th, water was discharged through 6 double hydrants, making 12 openings of 2½ inches; time of this test two hours and forty-five minutes, the pumps, at this rate of speed, pumping more than 1,000,000 gallons over contract requirements.]

FIRE DEPARTMENT KALAMAZOO, Oct. 1, 1877

W. S. Dewing, Esq., Chairman of Committee on Fire and Water:

SIR—By your order I made a fire test of the Worthington Pumps, on Friday, September 28th, commencing at 9 o'clock A. M., and lasting forty-five minutes. Gates were closed around the district where streams were thrown. Points from which streams were thrown are as follows:

Corner of	Burdick	and	South	Streets,	1¼	inch nozzle.
"	"	"	Main	"	1⅛	" "
"	"	"	Lovell	"	1⅛	" "
"	"	"	Water	"	1⅛	" "
"	Lovell	"	Rose	"	1	" "
"	Rose	"	Main	"	1¼	" "
"	Main	"	Portage	"	1	" "
"	"	"	Edwards	"	1	" "
"	Burdick	"	Main	"	1⅛	" "
"	Kalamazoo Ave.	"	Edwards	"	1	" "
Opposite	Merrill & Mc Courtie's Elevator				1⅛	" "

In all, ten first-class fire streams were thrown at an average height of over one hundred feet, and I have no doubt more streams could have been thrown, still sustaining the same height of water.

The above report is respectfully submitted.

THOS. O'NEILL, Chief Engineer.

[It is worthy of remark, when the streams were reduced to three, the height of water thrown was over 140 feet and when cut down to one stream the height of water thrown was 188 feet.]

The Worthington Duplex Pumping Engine, on motion, was accepted, and the members of the Board expressed themselves as fully satisfied in every way with the manner in which Mr· Worthington had fulfilled his part of the contract.

Recommendation was made "that Fire Extinguishers be placed in each of the school houses in the Village," and the Chairman of the Committee on Fire and Water was instructed to consult with the Board of Education in reference to it.

1878—APRIL 15. A report was made by the special committee appointed April 20, 1877, on "repairing and keeping in repair Corporation Hall," in which was stated the action of such committee on repairing the hall proper, also a report of the changes made in the Fire Department (done with the knowledge and concurrence of the Fire and Water Committee); the Fire Department was in such condition as to call for radical changes and improvements to make it a convenient and efficient fire station. The construction of "trips" to be operated by the stroke of the gong, opening stall doors properly fitted with spring hinges, together with changes in the position of horses, etc., made a radical change in the time necessary to hitch up and get on the street. With the old appliances of the department it took from 40 to 60 seconds to get out; with the new arrangement it is always under 15 seconds.

[It is well here to note that the time of hitching is in most cases less than six seconds, and the time to be on the street less than 12 seconds. There have been some very important improvements made since the work of the special committee was closed and all such improvements have tended to increase the speed of hitching and operating the hose company, thereby increasing greatly its efficiency. About one mile of water pipe was laid during the past year, and the same supplied with all necessary hydrants, gates, etc.]

'78—Oct. 7. A change was made in the fire limits boundaries and a considerable addition made to the territory within the limits. The rules with reference to the construction of new buildings, and the repair of all old buildings were made still more stringent in their nature. The Committee on Fire and Water were instructed to see such rules duly enforced as contemplated by the ordinance.

'78—Dec. 2. A remonstrance was submitted to the Board of Trustees praying for a change in the boundaries of the new fire limits, and, on motion, a portion of the limits as established Oct. 7, was excluded, mainly on the ground of creating too great hardship on property owners in the outer districts.

1879—March 3. The fire limits again changed to exclude more territory, being on north side of East Main street included in the limits as established, Oct. 7, 1878.

'79—April 28. Fred. Cellem appointed Water Commissioner at a salary of $400, continuing in office one year.

'79—June 5. The Committee on Fire and Water, through their Chairman T. R. Bevans, submitted a report with reference to the necessity of providing a second line of water mains from the Water Works, representing the inadequacy of the Burdick street 10 inch main to supply sufficient water if any further extensions were made of water mains, together with the danger of trusting to one line of piping from the works, as, in case of a breakage, the Village would be totally destitute of water supply. After considerable discussion the report of the committee was adopted, and the committee authorized to lay a new 10 inch main from the Water Works to supply the lines of pipe (about two miles in length) proposed in the report of the committee. They were also authorized to purchase and lay the full amount of water pipe as reported.

'79—Sept. 1. The Committee on Fire and Water reported the completion of the water main construction for the year, and that the whole matter of work and material had been entirely satisfactory to the committee.

'79—Sept. 27. A special committee of three was appointed to examine into the matter of "fire limits," and the ordinance relating thereto, known as No. 12, and to report any desirable change in such, either on regulations or boundaries.

'79—Oct. 23.   The special committee on Fire Limit Ordinance No. 12, made a full report on the subject recommending some radical changes, both as to its provisions and boundaries.   After a great deal of discussion and various amendments, the ordinance was passed and ordered printed.

'79—Nov. 6.   An alarm of fire was sounded at 1:30 A. M., and was found to be on Portage street, at the Bending Works.   In consequence of the inflamability of the material contained in the building it was impossible to save but a small portion of the property.

1880—March 1.   Under instructions from the Board, the Chief Engineer of the Fire Department made a sale to the Village of Schoolcraft of Hand Engine Excelsior No. 2, together with 100 feet of hose, for the sum of $500.00.

'80—May 4.   John D. Sumner appointed Water Commissioner, at a salary of $500, remaining in the position for nine months.

'80—Aug. 2.   Trustee Clarage, Chairman of Committee on Fire and Water, reported favorably on laying water pipe to the North-west School House, on Woodard avenue, and stated that the district proposed paying $100 toward the laying of same.

The committee was authorized to lay such pipe, with the condition of the payment of such amount by the district.

'80—Oct. 7.   A Knowles No. 3 pump, as a boiler feeder, was put in at the Water Works; it being considered dangerous to longer trust to one pump only.   Whole cost of pump and setting $286.

1881—April 4.   The Board of Trustees ratified the recent election of Hugh Beggs, as Chief, and Michael Blaney, as Assistant Chief Engineer of the Fire Department.

'81—April 14.   The following resolution was offered by Trustee Hill, and on motion was unanimously adopted:

"Whereas, By the appointment of Hugh Beggs, Chief of the Fire Department, at our meeting, April 4th, 1881, in the place of Thomas O'Neill, we lose the service of one who has faithfully and continuously served this Village as fireman from 1860, and as Chief of the Department continuously since 1866: therefore,

"Resolved, That the thanks of this Board are tendered to our late Chief of the Fire Department, Thomas O'Neill, for his long, faithful and efficient services in that responsible position, and we take pleasure in certifying to his good judgment, conscientious and fearless discharge of duty at all times.

"RESOLVED, That the Village Clerk furnish Mr. O'Neill a certified copy of these resolutions.

"Kalamazoo, April 14th, 1881."

[The certified copy of these resolutions was sent to Mr. O'Neill on the 29th day of April 1881.]

'81—APRIL 18.   James W. Hopkins was appointed Water Commissioner, at a salary of $500, and Geo. H. Chandler was again appointed Chief Engineer of the Water works, and Chas. Healy, Assistant Chief.   No changes were made in the members of the Paid Fire Department.

MACHINERY
—AT—
THE WATER WORKS.

The machinery, first put into the Water Works, in 1869, was as follows:

One engine frame, arched at an angle of 90°, height 8 feet 4 inches; length of base 18 feet 2½ inches; width of same 5 feet 4 inches.

Two steam cylinders 14 by 24 inches fastened on one side of the frame, at an angle of 45°; connection rods attached, by one crank pin, to one end of main shaft; air pump and "boiler feed-pump," worked by a crank, at the opposite end of same shaft.

One condenser elevated twenty inches above floor line; steam cut-off at ¾ of stroke and regulated by "Holly's Hydrostatic Regulator."

The engines changed from low to high pressure by opening the exhaust valves, either capable of being run separately.   One steam Donkey pump for boiler feed, when large engines were still.

Two No. 12 Rotary pumps (mounted on iron frames and standing on the curb of the pumping well,) to which the power was transmitted by gearing; two suction pipes extending directly down into the well; the discharge pipes extending upward, and when united, curving downward to connect with the street main.   Each pump was rated at a capacity of 1,000,000 gallons in twenty-four hours—the contract providing that pumps and engines should be of a capacity to discharge 2,000,000 gallons in the same time and to throw six one inch streams to a perpendicular height of one hundred feet.

Two upright fire box boilers of seven feet outside diameter and six feet high, with 530 hanging flues 22 inches in length and 1½ inches in diameter; guaranteed to raise steam, from cold water, in ten minutes, from the time of putting fire under the boilers. Each boiler was furnished with a sheet iron stack and an artificial draft was created, by a fan, for each ash pit.

In March, 1870, the first condenser was replaced by a new and larger one; and during the summer a brick smoke stack was built.

In July of the same year a steam Rotary Engine was added.

In April, 1871, one of the rotary pumps was broken and sent to Lockport, N. Y., for repairs; a new pump was purchased to take its place; and the broken pump, when repaired, was returned and kept as a reserve.

In the summer of 1872, a new horizontal boiler, made by Kimball, Austin & Co., took the place of one the original upright boilers; it was 72 inches in diameter and 14 feet long, with 78 four inch flues.

In June, 1873, two new piston pumps, of a duty capacity of 1,000,000 gallons in twenty-four hours, were bought of the Holly Manufacturing Co.; and in October they were working satisfactorily

In December following, a Knowles' Pony Feed Pump, No. 3, took the place of the original boiler feed pump; and at the same time, the engines were changed to non-condensing, which was a grave mistake.

In November, 1874, another horizontal boiler, 60 inches in diameter and 14 feet long, with 78 three inch flues, was added.

In July, 1875, a Stillwell Heater and Lime Extractor took the place of the old surface condenser.

In November, of the same year, all boilers were repaired.

In the summer of 1877, the old steam Rotary Engine and the Rotary Pumps were removed, and the capacity of the Water Works was greatly increased by the introduction of one "High Pressure Duplex Pumping Engine" furnished by H. R. Worthington, of New York, of a capacity of 2,000,000 gallons in twenty-four hours, at 78 strokes per minute, against a head of 250 feet. This engine consisted of two steam engines of 29 inches inside diameter, $25\frac{1}{2}$ inches stroke and two water plungers 15 inches in diameter and $25\frac{1}{2}$ inches stroke.

In October, 1880, another Knowles Feed Pump No. 3, was added.

INVENTORY OF WATER WORKS.

The machinery now in use April, 1881, consists of:

One Holly Pumping Engine of a capacity of 1,000,000 gallons in twenty-four hours.

One Worthington high-pressure "duplex pumping engine" of a capacity of 2,000,000 gallons in twenty-four hours.

One horizontal boiler 72 inches in diameter and 14 feet long.

One horizontal boiler 60 inches in diameter and 14 feet long.

One Holly upright boiler 7 feet in diameter and 6 feet high.

Two No. 3 Knowles boiler feed pumps; and one Stillwell Heater and Lime Extractor No. 7; and

All in good working order.

TABLE "D."

SHOWING LOCATION OF WATER MAINS WITH SIZE IN INCHES AND LENGTH IN FEET.

STREET.	DIAMETER OF PIPE.								TOTAL.
	2 inch.	3 inch.	4 inch.	6 inch.	8 inch.	10 inch.	12 inch.	16 inch.	
Academy	1,485								1,485
Burdick			1,886	2,640	1,089	2,882			8,497
Burr Oak				18		1,163			1,181
Cedar			1,056	1,716					2,772
Cherry			789						789
Dutton	680		468	630					1,778
Eleanor			662						662
Elm	472								472
Edwards			818						818
First			689						689
Henrietta	417								417
Jackson			700						700
John			924						924
Kalamazoo Avenue			6,040						6,040
Locust			1,650						1,650
Lovell			4,803						4,803
Lake	85		882						967
Main		583	4,780	2,574					7,923
North			1,320						1,320
Park			2,310		1,542				3,852
Pitcher	176		535						711
Porter			396						396
Portage		400	4,101						4,501
Potts Avenue				64					64
Rose			2,672	798					3,470
Ransom			1,782						1,782
South	825		3,069						3,894
Stuart Avenue			1,122						1,122
Vine			3,366						3,366
Walnut	660		2,172						2,832
Water	228		486	618					1,332
West			1,404	4,105					5,509
Willard			396						396
Woodward Avenue			2,024						2,024
Wheaton			726						726
Blount's Alley			272						272
Dudgeon Alley			198						198
Lateral Pipe			3,250						3,250
Discharge at Works							18	8	26
Suction at Works					30	36		117	183
TOTAL	5,028	969	57,748	13,163	2,661	4,081	18	125	83,793

Total Pipe of all sizes—15 miles and 4,593 feet.

TABLE "E."

LOCATION OF FIRE HYDRANTS.

Alley opposite Dewing's office.
Burdick street, east side near Water Works.
Burdick street, east side, opposite Burr Oak.
Burdick street, northeast corner Vine.
Burdick street, northeast corner Dutton.
Burdick street, northeast corner Walnut.
Burdick street, east side, opposite Cedar.
Burdick street, southeast corner Lovell.
Burdick street, northeast corner South.
Burdick street, west side, at Corporation Hall.
Burdick street, southeast corner Main.
Burdick street, southeast corner Water.
Burdick street, east side, near Eleanor.
Burdick street, northeast corner Kalamazoo ave.
Burdick street, northwest cor. alley at No. 3 Hose House.
Burdick street, east side, north of M. C. R. R. freight house.
Burdick street, northwest corner Ransom.
Burdick street, northeast corner North.
Burdick street, northwest corner Frank.
Burdick street, southeast corner Parsons.
Burdick street, northeast corner alley.
Burdick street, southeast corner Bush.
Burr Oak street, southeast corner Burr Oak and Rose.
Burr Oak street, southeast corner Burr Oak and Park.
Church street, northeast corner Ransom.
Church street, southwest corner Kalamazoo ave.
Church street, northeast corner Main.
Cooley street, northwest corner Kalamazoo ave.
Cherry street, south side, opposite Edward.
Dutton street, northwest corner John.
Edward street, southwest corner Dewing's alley.
Edward street, northeast corner Dewing's engine room.
Edward street, west side, north of Arcadia.
Eleanor street, north side, bet. Rose and Burdick.
First street, southwest corner Acker.
Jackson street, north side, near Merrill & McCourtie's mill.
John street, southeast corner Walnut.
John street, southeast corner East Cedar.
Kalamazoo avenue, northwest corner Edward.
Kalamazoo avenue, northwest corner Pitcher.
Kalamazoo avenue, northwest corner Porter.
Kalamazoo avenue northwest corner Waldbridge.
Kalamazoo avenue, southwest corner Woodward avenue.
Kalamazoo avenue, northwest corner Elm.
Kalamazoo avenue, north side of 'Short.'
Lake street, north side, opposite brewery.
Lake street, north side, opposite school house.
Locust street, northwest corner Vine.
Locust street, west side, bet. Vine and Walnut.
Locust street, northwest corner Walnut.
Locust street, northwest corner Cedar.
Locust street, southwest corner Lovell.
Lovell street, southeast corner Henrietta.
Lovell street, southwest corner Jasper.
Lovell street, south side, center of Church.
Lovell street, southwest corner Potter alley.
Lovell street, southwest corner Davis.
Lovell street, southeast corner Asylum avenue.
Main street, south side, near junction of Kalamazoo avenue.
Main street, northeast corner Porter.
Main street, southeast corner Pitcher.
Main street, northwest corner Edwards.
Main street, southeast corner Portage.
Main street, south side, between Portage and Burdick.
Main street, north side, front of Burdick House.
Main street, south side, front of L. L. Clark's.
Main street, on west corner Michigan avenue.
Main street, northwest corner Woodward avenue.
Main street, north side, between Park and West.
Main street, northwest corner Stuart avenue.

Main street, west side, near Douglas avenue.
Main street, southeast corner Thompson.
North street, northeast corner Edwards.
North street, southeast corner Pitcher.
North street, northwest corner Porter.
Oak street, northeast corner Vine.
Oak street, southwest corner Walnut.
Oak street, southwest corner Cedar.
Oak street, southwest corner Lovell.
Park street, southeast corner Vine.
Park street, southwest corner Dutton.
Park street, northeast corner Walnut.
Park street, northwest corner Cedar.
Park street, southwest corner Lovell.
Park street, southwest corner South.
Park street, southwest corner Academy.
Park street, southwest corner Main.
Park street, northeast corner Eleanor.
Park street, northwest corner Kalamazoo avenue.
Park street, southwest corner Ransom.
Pitcher street, northwest corner Cherry.
Pearl street, southeast corner Walnut.
Pearl street, northwest corner Cedar.
Portage street, northeast corner Cherry.
Portage street, southeast corner Spring.
Portage street, northeast corner Lovell.
Portage street, southeast corner First.
Portage street, southeast corner Third.
Portage street, southeast corner Vine.
Portage street, southeast corner Jackson.
Portage street, northeast corner Lake.
Rose street, east side, opposite No. 85 South Rose.
Rose street, southeast corner Vine.
Rose street, southwest corner Dutton.
Rose street, southeast corner Walnut.
Rose street, southwest corner Cedar.
Rose street, southeast corner Lovell.
Rose street, southwest corner South.
Rose street, southeast corner Academy.
Rose street, southwest corner Main.
Rose street, northwest corner Water.
Rose street, northeast corner Eleanor.
Rose street, northwest corner Eleanor.
Rose street, northwest corner Kalamazoo avenue.
Rose street, northeast corner Willard.
Rose street, southwest corner Ransom.
South street, southwest corner Henrietta.
South street, three hydrants 20 rods apart west of West.
Stuart avenue, northwest corner Kalamazoo ave.
Stuart avenue, west side, and north of Chas. E. Stuart's.
Walnut street, southeast corner Potter.
Walnut street, north side, opposite hay market.
Water street, northwest corner Edward.
West street, southwest corner Wheaton avenue.
West street, southwest corner Village.
West street, northwest corner Vine.
West street, southwest corner Dutton.
West street southeast corner Walnut.
West street, northwest corner Cedar.
West street, southwest corner Lovell.
West street, southwest corner South.
West street, southeast corner Academy.
West street, southwest corner Main.
West street, northeast corner Water.
West street, northeast corner Eleanor.
West street, northeast corner Kalamazoo avenue.
West street, northeast corner Willard.
West street, northeast corner Ransom.
Wheaton avenue, opposite No. 21.
Woodward avenue, opposite Elmwood street.
Woodward avenue opposite school house.
Vine street, west end of street on Davis.
Willard street, north side, in front M. C. R. R. depot.
"Bush & Patterson's," one hydrant at the northwest corner of engine room.
Total number, 147.

TABLE "F."
WATER GATES. SIZE AND LOCATION.

STREETS.	2 inch.	4 inch.	6 inch.	8 inch.	10 inch.
Academy. West line of Park street	1				
" West line of West street	1				
" East line of West street	1				
Burdick. At Water Works					2
" At Water Works		1			
" Opposite Burr Oak street		1			
" North line of Vine street					1
" At hydrant on northeast corner Vine street			1		
" At hydrant on northeast corner Dutton street			1		
" At hydrant on northeast corner Walnut street			1		
" Northeast corner Dutton street			1		
" North line Cedar street				1	
" 4 feet south of hydrant on Cedar street					1
" 5 feet from hydrant on Cedar street		1			
" 11 feet from hydrant on Cedar street			1		
" 11 feet from hydrant on Main street			1		
" Gate to cistern on Main street			1		
" South line of Water street			1		
" South line of Kalamazoo avenue			1		
" South line of Willard street			1		
" North line of Eleanor street			1		
" North line of Frank street			1		
" East line of Frank street	1				
" By No. 3 Hose House			2		
Burr Oak. Opposite Rose street				1	
" Southeast cor Rose street				1	
Cedar. West line of West street				1	
" East line of West street				1	
Cherry. Southeast corner Portage street			2		
" Northwest corner Pitcher street	1				
Dutton. West line of Rose street	1				
" Southwest corner Park street			1		
Edwards, North line of Water street			1		
Henrietta. Southwest corner South street	1				
Jackson. East line of Portage street			1		
John. South line of Lovell street			1		
" North of hydrant at Walnut street	1				
Kalamazoo ave. West line of Burdick street			1		
" East line of Burdick street			1		
" West line of West street			1		
" East line of West street			1		
" East line of Edwards street			1		
Lovell. East line of Burdick street			1		
" West line Rose street			1		
" West line of Park street			1		
" West line of West street			1		
" East line of Henrietta street	1				
" Northwest corner Davis street			1		
Locust. South line of Walnut street			1		
" South line Lovell street			1		
Main. 28 feet east and 20 feet west curb at Portage st.			1		
" Gate to cistern at Portage street		1			
" 18 feet east and 4 feet north curb at Portage st.			1		
" 10 feet west of west curb on Burdick street			1		
" Gate to cistern at Burdick street		1			
" East curb of Burdick street			1		
" West line Rose street			1		
" East line of West street			1		
" West line of West street		1			
" West line of Stuart avenue			1		
North. East line of Ransom street			1		
Park. North line of Cedar street			1		
" South line of Cedar street			1		
" North line of South street			1		
" Opposite Burr Oak street					1
" Opposite Burr Oak street				1	
" Southwest corner Dutton street				1	
" Center of Vine street			1		
Portage. 14 feet north of Cherry street			1		
" South line of Lovell street			1		
" South line of Lovell street		1			
" South of hydrant at Lake street		1			
" Southeast corner First street			1		
" At Lake street			1		
" At Lake street		1			
Pine. Southeast corner Pine street		1			
Rose. North line of Vine street			1		

WATER GATES. (CONTINUED.)

STREETS.		2 inch.	4 inch.	6 inch.	8 inch.	10 inch.
Rose.	North line of Cedar street.............................	....	1	....	....	....
"	South line of Cedar street.............................	....	1	....	....	....
"	North line of Academy street.........................	....	1	....	....	....
Ransom.	West line of Burdick street............................	....	1	....	....	....
"	East line of West street................................	....	1	....	....	....
South.	East line of Burdick street........	....	1	....	....	....
"	West line of Rose street.............................	....	1	....	....	....
"	North edge of south sidewalk in Park..........	1	....	....	....	....
"	West line of Park street.............................	1	....	....	....	....
"	West line of West street	....	....	1	....	....
"	East line of West street..............................	1	....	....	....	....
Stuart avenue.	North line of Main street............................	....	1	....	....	....
Vine.	West line of Burdick street.........................	....	....	....	1	....
"	West line of West street.............................	....	....	1	....	....
Water.	East line of Burdick street...........................	....	....	....	1	....
Walnut.	East line of Burdick street...........................	....	....	1	....	....
"	West line of Rose street.............................	1	....	....	....	....
"	East line of Park street..............................	1	....	....	....	....
"	East line of West street..............................	....	....	1	....	....
"	West line of West street............................	....	1	....	....	....
Willard	West line of Burdick street.........................	....	1	....	....	....
Woodward ave.	North line of Main street	....	1	....	....	....
"	North line of Kalamazoo avenue..................	....	1	....	....	....
West.	Opposite Dutton street..............................	....	1	....	....	....
"	Northwest corner Vine street......................	....	1	1	....	....
"	Southwest corner Wheaton avenue	....	1	....	....	....
	TOTAL..	18	64	17	3	5

Total number of Gates, 107.

TABLE "G."

PUMPING RECORD OF THE KALAMAZOO WATER WORKS FOR THE YEAR ENDING
MARCH 31st, 1881.

MONTH.	Days run of 24 Hours.		Gallons Pumped.	Daily Average.	Pressure on Guage.	Height in Feet.	No of times Water Pressure raised to 100lbs for Fires.	No. of times Water Pressure raised to 90lbs for L. C. Chapin.	No. of times Water Pressure raised to 90lbs for Cemetery.	No. minutes Works not run each month.	No. of inches Water lowered in Well.
	Holly Engine.	Worthington Engine.									
April.................1880	27	3	16,934,400	564,480	45	102	2	2	6	....	18
May........... "	31	1	19,998,720	645,120	45	102	1	6	1	....	19
June .... "	28	2	23,012,600	767,080	45	102	2	4	5	....	20
July................... "	28	3	26,279,320	847,720	50	113–13	2	4	8	....	24
August............... "	23	8	27,529,240	888,040	50	113–13	1	6	10	....	30
September........... "	29	1	26,035,200	867,840	50	113–13	....	3	5	....	29
October .... "	31	......	25,028,160	807,360	50	113–13	....	2	....	....	23
November .... "	27	3	23,616,000	787,200	45	102	2	3	1	....	20.
December .... "	29	2	26,178,080	847,680	45	102	3	3	....	....	24
January..............1881	29	2	30,027,850	968,640	45	102	1	2	....	....	36
February............. "	25	3	25,992,960	928,320	50	113–13	7	....	1	....	34
March .... "	30	1	22,537,620	727,020	45	102	....	3	....	14	19½
TOTAL......	336	29	293,269,940	....	......	....	21	38	43	14	....

Daily average of water pumped for the year, 803,468 gallons.
Wood consumed in 12 months, 1,092 3-16 cords.
Average cost of wood per cord, including freight and extra labor, $2,338.
Wood consumed in 24 hours, 2,992 cords.
Cost of wood for 24 hours run, $7,005.
Cost of fuel used in raising 1,000,000 gallons of water 100 feet high, $7,23.
The average daily cost of maintainance of Water Works, including the permanent improvements,
is $18,788.

CLOSING CHAPTER.

RECAPITULATION OF INVENTORY.

Three village lots, and the buildings thereon.

Machinery and foundations.

Water mains, 83,793 feet—(15 miles and 4,593 feet.)

Hydrants, 147. Gates, 107.

APPRAISEMENT

Your committee have made, with great care, an appraisement of the present value of the Water Works property, thus inventoried, and report:

Real estate, Water Works buildings, coal and wood sheds, Engineer's
    residence, barn, etc.,...$ 5,000

Machinery and foundations,......... 25,000

Water Mains (83,793 feet); Hydrants (147); Gates (107), labor, lead,
    freight, incidentals; (first cost of which was $107,437.79)............ 99,750

Water Works Well, (first cost $10,343) 10,000

Fire Alarm Gong, tools and implements... 250

Total appraised value of Water Works and appurtenances,............$140,000

The property belonging to the Fire Department, has been likewise appraised, as follows:

Hose carts and hose; hooks, ladders and trucks;

Horses, harness and implements;

Fire Alarm Telegraph and instruments.

Appraised present value of Fire Department property........................$ 5,000

Total appraisment of all property in Fire and Water Department....$145,000

ANALYSIS OF FINANCIAL TABLES.

Calling attention to the Financial Tables, which follow, it is proper to remark, that they have been prepared with extreme care and are the result of much labor.

Tables 1 and 2, combined, show that the total cost of the Water Works for *construction* and for *current expenses*, for the twelve years of their existence, has been $255,902.65.

While it is relatively easy to show this, it is not so easy to show, exactly, how much of this total cost is chargeable to "construction account" and how much to "expense account." The rea-

son for this is found in the fact, that, in the earlier years of the
Water Works history, the orders, drawn on the Village Treasury,
often failed to specify whether the amount, so ordered to be paid,
was chargeable to "construction" or to "expense." The bills and
vouchers of each year, therefore, have been carefully scrutinized
and their several amounts have been charged, to "construction" or
to "running expense," as circumstances seemed to warrant. This
difficulty is particularly noticable in the items carried to "Freight"
and to "Incidentals;" but your committee have exercised their best
judgment in carrying these doubtful items to their proper place.

It is also difficult to determine, exactly, the proportion of Water
Commissioner's salary to be charged to each account. Some of it is
certainly chargeable to "construction," but *how* much must be a
matter of judgement. In the following analysis it is all charged to
"running expense."

With this explanation, we give the cost of

CONSTRUCTION OF WATER WORKS.

Real Estate, Buildings, etc.,..$	8,450 18
New Machinery..	43,432 99
Freight and Incidentals chargeable thereto......................	4,872 28
Pipe, Hydrants, Gates, Lead, etc....................................	71,145 16
Freight and Incidentals chargeable thereto......................	10,734 30
Labor laying Pipes, Hydrants and Gates..........................	20,195 62
Water Works Well...	10,343 00
TOTAL COST OF CONSTRUCTION................................ $	168,673 53
Appraised present value of the property...........................	140,000 00
Estimated loss by changes and wear, in 12 years................ $	28,673 53

Average annual loss by changes and wear, $2,389 46.

[It should not be overlooked or forgotten, that a large part of
this "loss" is due to changes, made to rectify early mistakes and to
increase the pumping capacity of the works, so as to supply increased population and demand.]

RUNNING EXPENSES OF WATER WORKS.

The total cost of the Water Works, for 12 years, is shown by Tables 1 and 2, to have been..	$255,902 65
If from this, we deduct "cost of construction"...................	168,673 53
We have a TOTAL "CURRENT EXPENSE," for 12 years, of.......... $	87,229 12
Average annual cost, $7,269 09.	
But the receipts from Water Rates, for 12 years, are............. $	40,034 65
NET RUNNING EXPENSE for 12 years................................ $	47,194 47

Net yearly average, $3,932 87.

FIRE DEPARTMENT PROPERTY.

Table 3 shows that the property of the Fire Department, under the
headings of "General Supplies" and "Telegraph Fire Alarm,"
cost, for 12 years... $ 14,154 73
Under the head of "Appraisement" this property, now in use, is
valued at.. 5,000 00

Total depreciation and loss, in 12 years............................... $ 9,154 73
To this add "Salaries," "Repairs," and "Incidentals," (Table 3)... 32,858 97

Net average annual cost of Fire Department, for 12 years....... $ 42.013 70

Net average annual cost of Fire Department,................$3,501 14
   "   "   "   "   running Water Works.......... 3,932 87
   "   "   "   loss on Water Works Property......... 2,389 46
   "   "   "   COST OF FIRE PROTECTION.............$9,823 47

The population of Kalamazoo is, now, about 13,000, occupying
over two thousand homes; and there is owned, within our corporate
limits, an amount of destructible and insurable property equal in
value to, at least, $3,500,000.00. (This estimate of property, des-
tructible by fire, has been very carefully made.) The net average
annual cost, for Fire Protection, for the last twelve years, is less,
therefore, than $\frac{1}{3}$ (but little over $\frac{1}{4}$) of one per cent. per annum, *on
the value of our insurable property*. (It should be borne in mind,
that land, lots, money, bonds, stocks, mortgages and other uninsura-
ble property, (nearly all taxable) are not taken into account, in this
calculation of the percentage of annual cost of Fire Protection on
our insurable property.)

Nor is this all. The efficiency of our Water Works and of our
Fire Department is greatly increased, and that too with decreas-
ed expense. For example: the total cost of running the Water
Works, during the last year, was $6,857,71, and receipts from
Water Rates and other credits were $5,422.89;

Making the net cost of running the works only.............................$1,434 82
If to this be added the cost of the Fire Department for 1880–81......... 4,311 67

We have..$5,746 49

as the net cost of Fire Protection for the last municipal year. This
sum, compared with the annual average of $9,823.47, for twelve
years, conclusively demonstrates that increased efficiency is compati-
ble with increased economy in this important part of our municipal expenditure.

It is now in order to remark; that none of the various plans of
water supply, ever offered or advocated for Kalamazoo, could have

been constructed with as little cost as our present system has been. No plan, but the one in use, could, by any possibility, have furnished *pure water and plenty of it.* No plan, but the one in use, could be made efficient, for fire protection, without the costly intervention and use of Steam Fire Engines, or some other equally expensive expedient. Saying nothing of the cost of water supply, two Steam Fire Engines cannot be run, by a Fire Department, in our Village, for $9,823.47, which is the net annual average cost, for the past twelve years, of our entire Fire Department, Water Works and all. And yet we grumble!

"But," it is said, "this estimate takes no account of the (nearly) $170,000 which we have invested in the Water Works, on which we get no interest or income." If, as remarked in our "Intermediate Chapter," we give the Water Works Fund an annual credit of $7,500 for the use of hydrants, for fire purposes, the Fund will give us 4½ per cent. (nearly) of annual interest on our first investment. If this investment had been made by a private corporation, we would have found out, long since, that the $7,500 per annum would have been estimated *by it and paid by us.* Many of us reason, or talk rather, about our Water Works much like the man who claimed that the house, he owned and lived in, paid him no interest on the cost of it. He moved out, leased it, and then rented another, for twice as much, to live in. It could not be considered good economy—but, he got rent for his house!

If Kalamazoo should move out of her own Water Works, and rent Water Works of a corporation, it easy to imagine the financial result. But it is also easy to imagine that she would not, willingly, be long a tenant, for the sake of getting rent on her property or interest on her investment.

TOTAL COST.

A careful search, of the early records of the Village, shows that it is now impossible to state, accurately, the cost of the Fire and Water Department, during the twenty-six years intervening between 1843, (when Kalamazoo became an incorporated village,) and 1869, when the Water Works were introduced; but enough has been found to show, that the approximate expense, for a Fire and Water Department, was,

During the 1st Municipal Period, of 26 years,............................. $ 25,000 00
Total expense for the 2d Municipal Period, of 12 years,................ 302,916 35

   Total expense for Fire and Water for 38 years...................... $327,916 35
Deducting receipts from Water Rates,..................................... 40,034 65

   Gives net expense for Fire and Water, for 38 years............... $287,881 70

Appraised value of property on hand....................................... $145,000 00

FIRE DEPARTMENT.

It only remains to say, that our present efficient Fire Department consists of six regular paid firemen, and of a volunteer force of fifteen men, belonging to Vigilant Hose Company No. 3.

The Paid Department has four horses, one horse hose cart, one hook and ladder truck, one hand engine, two Babcock extinguishers, and all the required equipments.

The volunteer force has one hand hose cart and equipments, also two hand hose carts not now in use.

The Paid Department is "always ready" and "never dilatory." Since its organization, we have had no serious losses, when the fire was near to the Water Mains and Hydrants. The volunteer force, when needed, is always efficient and useful.

The effective power of our Water Works, as controlled by its engineers and applied by the Fire Department, to the extinguishment of fire, is well attested by the relatively small losses by fire, during the last nine years, as reported by the Chief Engineer of the Fire Department.

Besides this, our homes, and our places of business, and our industries, are all supplied, at small cost, with an abundance of pure, wholesome water.

In conclusion: We have gone carefully over the record of the Fire and Water interests, enterprises and expenditures of Kalamazoo, from April 1843, when it became a village, till April, 1881. We have sought to report fully, but tersely, every fact of importance in all this history. We have paused, occasionally, to comment on interesting and important events, but we have not sought to color the facts, or to report aught but the truth. We may be permitted to say, that our task has involved great labor; but it has been cheerfully and, we hope, well done. To the judgment of the power that appointed us and assigned to us our task, as well as to the judgement of all our fellow citizens, interested in the credit and prosperity of Kalamazoo, our work is now respectfully submitted.

FOSTER PRATT,

FRANK LITTLE,

FRED. CELLEM,

WILLIAM R. COATS,

GEORGE H. CHANDLER,

JAMES W. HOPKINS,

Committee.

www.ingramcontent.com/pod-product-compliance
Lightning Source LLC
Chambersburg PA
CBHW030715110426
42739CB00030B/580